Saving Bernice

Other titles in

THE NORTHEASTERN SERIES ON GENDER, CRIME, AND LAW

edited by Claire Renzetti, St. Joseph's University

Jody Raphael

Saving Bernice

BATTERED WOMEN,

WELFARE,

AND POVERTY

Northeastern University Press

BOSTON

Northeastern University Press 2000

LIBRARY OF CONGRESS CATALOGING-IN-PUBLICATION DATA

Raphael, Jody.
  Saving Bernice : battered women, welfare, and poverty / Jody Raphael.
      p.   cm.—(The Northeastern series on gender, crime, and law)
  Includes bibliographical references and index.
  ISBN 1–55553–439–2 (alk. paper)—ISBN 1–55553–438–4
  (pbk. : alk. paper)
      1. Abused women—United States.   2. Welfare recipients—
  Abuse—United States.   3. Public welfare—United States.
  4. Family violence—United States.   I. Title.   II. Series.
  HV6626.2.R37   2000
  362.82'928'0973—dc21   99-088074

Designed by Diane Gleba Hall

Composed in Joanna by Coghill Composition Company in Richmond,
Virginia. Printed and bound by Edwards Brothers, Inc., in Ann Arbor,
Michigan. The paper is EB Natural, an acid-free sheet.

MANUFACTURED IN THE UNITED STATES OF AMERICA
04   03   02   01   5   4   3   2

Contents

For Paul and Sheila Wellstone, and Claire Renzetti, my very first reader

Acknowledgments

I will always be grateful to Bernice Hampton, who has entrusted the telling of her story to me. That she was willing to do so was a touching sign of faith that has sustained me through the several years of writing this book. Although I experienced some of her story along with Bernice, she agreed to sit for about twelve two-hour taped interviews between 1995 and 1999. Early on, it became apparent that these sessions caused Bernice to relive the trauma she had earlier experienced, but Bernice persevered because she hoped the "soul-gripping" project, as she put it, would continue to be a healing aid to some of her pain, and, most importantly, would also help educate others about the challenges battered women on welfare face.

The first draft of this book was written while I was a visiting fellow at the University of Oxford Centre for Cross-Cultural Research on Women. I greatly benefited from conversations with members of the Centre and from attending stimulating research workshops and lectures. I am particularly grateful to the center's director, Catherine Lloyd, who took a personal interest in my work and guided me to a number of important theoretical works that influenced my thinking.

Claire Renzetti, the editor of the journal *Violence against Women*, has always believed that Bernice's story was one that should be told. She helped to make this book a reality with her great enthusiasm, steadfast encouragement, and expert editorial suggestions on all-too-numerous rough drafts. My collaborative work over the past three years with Rich Tolman at the University of Michigan School of Social Work has been crucial to the development of the ideas I present in this book, and I thank him for his insights as well as for his enthusiastic support. I have

viii   also benefited from the work of three additional scholars in this field: Lisa Brush, Stephanie Riger, and Joan Meier, who have generously shared their knowledge and ideas with me.

I am appreciative of the interest and support shown for this manuscript by Terri Teleen and Bill Frohlich of Northeastern University Press. Asa Soderman-Houston at the Press provided a close reading of the manuscript that pointed out many instances of inconsistencies and lack of clarity. Her perceptive editorial suggestions have greatly improved this book.

Many staff members at Center for Impact Research (formerly Taylor Institute) provided technical assistance with this book in its latter stages of preparation. I am most grateful to summer research associate Helene Marcy, who greatly helped, beyond the call of duty, with reference checking and construction of the bibliography.

Lastly, the encouragement of my family was crucial, especially the loving support of my husband, Alan.

Saving Bernice

Prologue: Giving Up the Secrets

> And so I go on to suppose that the shock-receiving capacity
> is what makes me a writer. I hazard the explanation that a
> shock is at once in my case followed by the desire to explain
> it. I feel that I have had a blow. . . . It is or will become a
> revelation of some order; it is token of some real thing
> behind appearance; and I make it real by putting it into
> words. It is only by putting it into words that I make it
> whole; this wholeness means that it has lost its power to
> hurt me.
>
> —VIRGINIA WOOLF, *Moments of Being*

In 1996 welfare reform represented the resolution of a highly polarized debate about the causes of women's poverty and dependence in the United States. Conservative analysts such as Charles Murray believed that receipt of welfare itself created a dependent class with no motivation to seek work, and as a result, the welfare system needed to be totally eliminated. [1] Other observers, such as Lawrence Mead, carefully analyzed welfare recipients and found them wanting to work but hopelessly burdened by a "culture of poverty," a state of mind conditioned by frequent failures that left women on welfare reluctant to try to make the transition from welfare to work. [2] The answer to this was, in his view, a mandatory work requirement—if one wanted women on welfare to work, one must expect and demand it.

Conservative commentators such as former vice president Dan

Quayle decried a welfare system that, by providing funds for unwed mothers and their children, supports single motherhood, encouraging the further breakdown of the nuclear family in the United States.[3] Although the basis or reasoning differed, the 1990s represented a broad-based consensus: we needed public policy that encouraged work, discouraged illegitimacy, and mandated that irresponsible fathers pay child support.

Many liberal welfare activists agreed that the welfare system was a failure. With its low benefit structure, women and children were reduced to living in conditions of extreme poverty.[4] Later it became apparent that indeed they could not live on welfare benefits alone and must develop other sources to supplement their benefits, from dependence on families and intimate partners to part-time or under-the-table work.[5] In the end, however, the national attack on welfare resulted in the demonization of low-income women as irresponsible—having children they could not support—and promiscuous.[6] The attack put many advocates, sincerely interested in the well-being of low-income women and their children, on the defensive.

Of course, there were a variety of responses to the perceived attack on single mothers. Some commentators, heroizing the single women who raised their children without the irresponsible men who had left them, advocated more adequate state support for them.[7] Others reasoned that low-income women did what was best for their children. Given their own low skills and the high cost of child care, the family was better off on welfare; to obtain a different result, one had to "make work pay," through education and job training opportunities leading to better paying jobs, increased minimum wage or earned income tax credits, an end to discrimination against women in the labor market, and affordable child care.[8]

Undoubtedly contributing to the polarization of the debate was one feminist response, holding that the welfare system was being attacked because it made it possible for women to support themselves and their children without men; thus the way women lived outside the nuclear family represented a healthy breakdown of the patriarchal way of life. It was, they reasoned, important for public policy to continue to supply and provide adequate benefits to these women, pioneers of new patterns of family life.[9]

It was indeed an irony that conservative supporters of the nuclear family were now advocating work outside the home for low-income women, while feminists, who might have been expected to encourage work for women, were advocating the right of the women to stay at home to raise their children. With the passage of the Personal Responsibility and Work Opportunity Reconciliation Act of 1996, work proponents won the day, with the act's sixty-month limit on federal welfare benefits and a requirement that women be involved in a work activity within twenty-four months.[10]

Unfortunately, the polarization of the debate made it impossible for either attackers or supporters of the welfare system to admit the elements of truth within each other's positions.[11] It is important to note, however, that all commentators were united in their world vision of welfare recipients, although they were hopelessly divided on the causes and the remedies: that is, that about four million (at the time) low-income women were living their lives as single mothers, raising their children without a man in the house. All policy debates took off from this starting point.

Beginning in 1995, research established for the first time that many women on welfare were current victims of domestic violence, whose intimate partners, threatened by their efforts at education, training, and employment, often sabotaged these activities by means of violence. Interviews with women documented the many ways that their partners interfered with welfare-to-work activities.[12] These included destruction of books and homework assignments; keeping women up all night with arguments before key tests or job interviews; inflicting visible facial injuries before job interviews; failing to show up as promised for child care or transportation for job interviews; and a host of additional abusive behaviors, including in-person harassment on the job that lead to their partners being fired. By 1997 quantitative research conclusively established that, although domestic violence is a factor in approximately 6 percent of all U.S. households, 20 to 30 percent of women receiving welfare are current victims of domestic violence—a considerable overrepresentation.[13]

Approaches to welfare reform, whether mandatory work or structural changes such as availability of affordable child care, may be doomed to failure, as some battered women are unable to comply with state work mandates or take advantage of new opportunities such as job training or child care. There are probably many possible scenarios.

6   Some domestic violence victims, unable to comply, will lose welfare
     benefits and remain more dependent on their abusing partner. Others
     may attempt to comply but face exacerbated domestic violence as a
     result, including severe injury or death. Some may find work but be
     unable to sustain the job owing to mental health issues that are the
     effects of the trauma. Still others will be able to seize the opportunity
     to find work and then escape their violent relationships. As there were
     approximately two million women on welfare in the United States in
     federal fiscal year 1998, the latest year for which there is available data,
     up to 400,000 women could experience these kinds of difficulties.[14]

         To explore all these issues, this book describes the responses one
     partner of a battered woman on welfare made to her efforts to obtain
     employment. Bernice Hampton's story illustrates how welfare and
     abuse trap battered women. At the time I met Bernice at the welfare-to-
     work program I was then directing, the twenty-six-year-old African
     American woman had two children, ages six and two. Bernice became
     a victim of domestic violence at the age of fourteen and applied for
     welfare at age eighteen. She became a welfare mother because she could
     not find a way to escape her intimate partner without grave injury, and
     he was unable to provide financially for her and their child. Bernice was
     trapped by the abuse: whenever she tried to go to training or get a job,
     which was often, her partner physically punished her. To go to work,
     Bernice would have to leave the relationship, but at the time she did
     not see a way to do so without risking her life. As most of the welfare
     money went to pay the monthly rent, Bernice was also trapped by
     poverty: her lack of funds further hampered her ability to devise a
     workable safety plan.

         So Bernice remained at home, trying to survive, sometimes living
     on as little as $361 a month. It took her three years to escape the vio-
     lence, and during the last year and a half she literally had to put her life
     on the line to do it. Today Bernice, thirty-three, and her children, ages
     thirteen and nine, are making a new life for themselves off welfare.

         In the last few years, advocates have embraced the new research
     about domestic violence and welfare by adding domestic violence to the
     ever-growing list of welfare-to-work barriers that need to be addressed,
     including low basic skills, alcohol and drug addiction, and lack of af-
     fordable child care or transportation. Welfare researchers have dutifully
     added domestic violence to the issues they would monitor or evaluate

in "welfare leaver" or welfare reform evaluation studies. However, the significance of the research on domestic violence and welfare, as exemplified by Bernice's story, continues to elude most poverty theorists. The large prevalence of domestic violence in the lives of welfare recipients challenges the fundamental assumptions of most welfare analysts, be they conservatives, liberals, or feminists. Data about domestic violence means that many women on welfare are not home alone and, as now seems commonsensical, are intimately involved with men. Many of these relationships are of long duration and involve the fathers of the women's children. Despite allegations to the contrary, low-income women and men have not rejected nuclear families; rather, it is the adherence to ideas of the nuclear family—and sexually ordained roles within them—that trap women in poverty.

Until recently, all sides in the welfare debate have resisted the full implications of this new information about violence and poverty, and it is not difficult to understand why. The existence of domestic violence makes the conservatives' mandatory work/"tough love" approach both ineffective and inappropriately harsh, with the potential for causing more violence. "Culture of poverty" theories, holding that welfare dependence or living in persistent poverty has sapped low-income persons' energy, causing depression, apathy, and helplessness, for which mandatory work is seen as the necessary antidote, crumble when confronted with a family problem such as domestic violence that cannot be remedied by mandatory work. The issue of domestic violence also challenges the major linchpin of feminist theory about women and welfare, that women are choosing to live outside the arrangements of the nuclear family and should be supported by the state. Domestic violence also undercuts the effectiveness of remedies many advocate such as reform of the labor market, child care provision, or "making work pay." If women's partners will not allow them into that workplace, all the structural changes, no matter how needed or important, will not be enough to bring about employment for some women on welfare. Lastly, to point to the beliefs, activities, or behavior of poor men in low-income women's lives as a fundamental cause of women's poverty appears to directly blame poor families for their problems, echoing the views of conservative welfare reformers.

By examining Bernice's story of domestic violence and welfare, this book draws on a single life to explain and explore the actions and

8   motivations of many poor battered women on welfare. Bernice's experiences illustrate the radically different kinds of assistance that need to be institutionalized in welfare-to-work policies. In addition, as Bernice's story illustrates, the issue of domestic violence can answer questions that have heretofore been simply inexplicable in antipoverty research. Why do poor girls and women continue to have babies they can't afford to support? Why do they not follow through or take advantage of education or training when it is offered? And why, despite all efforts to help them find employment, do some remain at home in poverty, even when they face the loss of welfare benefits?

The answers lie in the many ways that domestic violence works to constrain the choices and coerce the actions of low-income women. When the issue of domestic violence is squarely faced, we no longer can view many women on welfare as lazy or helpless, but instead we see young women like Bernice Hampton struggling to use birth control and trying to sustain employment in the teeth of their partners' violent opposition.

By moving from the myth of the single mother we have the opportunity to truly understand the role that intimate relationships play in perpetuating poverty. This work will thus undertake several critical explorations to advance our understanding of antipoverty strategies that now need to be employed as the result of the large prevalence of domestic violence within welfare households. Why is there more domestic violence in low-income households as compared to others? Why do so many women on welfare end up with abusive partners? Why are so many low-income men so threatened by their partners' self-sufficiency that they resort to violence? How do these attitudes serve to keep both men and women in poverty, at the margins of today's economy? And what is the public policy solution—what should be the government's role?

In the same way that the issue of domestic violence sheds light on the causes of women's poverty, the issue of domestic violence and welfare also provides us with new insights into the causes of domestic violence itself, as the domestic violence movement has, until recently, failed to focus on issues of race and class.[15] Historically, the battered women's movement has expressed as a fundamental creed that domestic violence is culturally taught and condoned, and that basic transformations in gender roles are required to eliminate it. The movement has long claimed that domestic violence occurs equally among all races and socioeconomic groups.[16] Confronting the higher prevalence of domestic violence within poor households might lead to a more nuanced and multidimensional view of batterers than we now have.[17] Bernice's story thus forces a critical synthesis of our theories about domestic violence causation with issues of economics or class, providing both new insights as well as more focused and effective interventions to end domestic violence.

But beyond all the new theory and policy insights about women's poverty that Bernice's story reveals, most important is the act of disclosure of the very issue of domestic violence itself. Domestic violence has been kept under wraps as a factor in welfare dependency mainly because the women themselves have kept it hidden. The violence in their lives is a matter of deep shame.

In a recent work, the writer Jill Nelson explains that black women have been largely silent about their lives as victims of violence. She says that this is the shameful secret that is kept: the greatest threat to the lives of black men is other black men, and the greatest violence visited on black women is by black men.

> There is one thing I know for sure; secrets are not healthy; they are always more trouble than they are worth. The act of keeping secrets eventually becomes all-consuming: the initial secret spawns lies created in order to protect the secret, which spawns bigger and more dangerous lies, and more secrets. By its very nature, the keeping of secrets presupposes the greater importance of those from whom the secrets are being kept, whoever they are. All the energy black women could and should spend transforming self and community and this nation is instead spent maintaining secrets, self-mutilation and victimization at its insidious best. In letting the secrets out, black women place ourselves in the center. Secrets, I have learned, gain power not in the telling, but in the keeping.[18]

In this book, Bernice now tells all her secrets, all the things she never revealed to a single soul. Understanding Bernice's story is a first step

10   toward building an effective antipoverty policy. Well-meaning policy makers on both sides of the political spectrum have forged ahead with policies, programs, and interventions based on official poverty statistics and mythology that do not comport with reality. And the secrets of poor women have remained buried.

CHAPTER ONE

Getting Trapped

In those days—the last of Queen Victoria—every house had
its Angel. And when I came to write I encountered her with
the very first words. The shadow of her wings fell on my
page; I heard the rustling of her skirts in the room. Directly,
that is to say, I took my pen in hand to review that novel by
a famous man, she slipped behind me and whispered: "My
dear, you are a young woman. You are writing about a book
that has been written by a man. Be sympathetic; be tender;
flatter; deceive; use all the arts and wiles of our sex. Never
let anybody guess that you have a mind of your own. Above
all, be pure." And she made as if to guide my pen. . . . I
turned upon her and caught her by the throat. I did my best
to kill her. My excuse, if I were to be had up in a court of
law, would be that I acted in self-defence. Had I not killed
her she would have killed me.

—VIRGINIA WOOLF, *"Professions for Women"*

It was no wonder that Bernice escaped her dysfunctional family the first
chance she got.[1] Bernice's father was an alcoholic who physically
abused his wife. One day he tied Bernice's thirteen-year-old brother
up, put him in a bucket, and poured gasoline and threw a match on
him, burning the youngster to death. He told her mother that if she
testified against him, he would kill her and all the other family members. Because of her fear Bernice's mother denied the truth on the wit-

12   ness stand. Bernice's aunt, however, told the truth in court. That day Bernice's father went home and shot at Bernice's mother seven times; he was shooting at Bernice's sister when her mother crawled down to the first floor to alert the neighbors.

Bernice's mother, pregnant with twins when she was shot, lost the babies and was in the hospital for eleven months. Her first husband, another alcoholic, came back to the family to help out. Bernice says her mother became an alcoholic after this violent incident. She and her first husband were drunk every day. Bernice's mother became violent when she drank, beat up her ex-husband constantly, shot at him, stabbed him, and neglected and abused her children when she was drunk, which was often.

Bernice was the baby in the family. She watched her three sisters escape the home by developing relationships with men. They weren't at home much, and when they did return they seemed as if they were happy. Bernice says she knows now that all three were involved in abusive relationships, but "all I saw was them away from Mom and Dad, away from the neighborhood, going to do something different, being around different people, and that was inviting to me."

When she was a freshman in high school Bernice met Billy, who was a junior at the school. Bernice was fourteen, and they dated secretly for a year before the relationship became intimate. Bernice thought Billy's family seemed normal. They ate together, they barbecued together, they went shopping together, and they had family reunions. Billy's mother didn't drink and his parents didn't fight.

> This was my first romance. It was a fantasy. It was like I was
> choosing another life. I didn't have to deal with the problems that
> were going on in my world. In the beginning we had love, closeness,
> and friendship. Billy fulfilled all my needs. I felt like I had his whole
> family watching out for me. I knew his family loved and cared for
> him, and they would accept, love, and protect me. I felt so connected
> and I felt safe. If my mother wanted to get abusive and violent with
> me, I could just go to him. I turned away from my family. I got
> tired of my family because I couldn't fix the problems there. I wanted
> to fix things and I couldn't, and so I escaped. Billy and his family
> were my escape.

At the time Billy seemed totally wrapped up in Bernice. Looking back
at it now, she sees the web of control that he was weaving even then.

> At age fourteen I wanted to be a teacher, and when I talked with
> him about it, he liked that idea. He said, "You know, if that is the
> career choice you want to do, you stick with your schooling," and
> he promoted whatever it was that made me feel good at fourteen years
> of age. It took years after that before he started to suppress my
> dreams. He agreed with my dreams as long as it was letting him
> into my life, but once he had gotten into my life, he pushed all my
> dreams out.

The violence didn't start until a year later. That spring, after Bernice's
freshman year, Billy told Bernice he was going to Michigan for two
weeks, but he didn't communicate or come back until the end of the
summer. When he returned, Billy wanted to take up where they had
left off, but Bernice wasn't willing. Billy grabbed Bernice and pushed
her against a wall. "He really hurt me, and I was so shocked, and I
thought I had better go ahead and do what he wants." Once they got
to his house Billy was back to his sweet, romantic self.

By the next summer the relationship had turned intimate, and Bernice began to talk about using birth control. Billy replied angrily that
girls who take birth control sleep around, and a really "big and ugly
fight" ensued. As a result of this dispute, Bernice went to a northern
suburb to stay with her sister for the summer. She did it to get away
from Billy; the relationship was "totally confusing" to her and she
wanted to escape to think about it.

Billy followed her there for visits. One time he took her to a nearby
park and forced sex on her there. Bernice was too ashamed to tell her
sister.

Several weeks later her sister was having a party and the group
wanted more drinks. She had given one of the guests some money to
go to the store with, but as she didn't want the guy to take off with her
money, her sister asked Bernice to accompany the man to the store.
They never went to the store. That Saturday night Bernice, at age fifteen,
was subjected to a second rape from this forty-year-old stranger.

Bernice told Billy about the rape. Billy's strong response—that he
would always love and protect her from others—convinced her to

renew her relationship with him. Billy told her that all men were like that, but that Bernice wouldn't have to worry about such things if she took him back. "I hid from the world with my relationship with Billy," Bernice explains today.

Bernice wanted to stay in school and wanted to use birth control, but she stopped talking about it because it was too much trouble. Billy would not countenance any use of birth control.

> *It wasn't a rational argument. I found it easier to give in to what he said. He threatened he would leave me. He brought the rape up constantly as a way of both demeaning me and scaring me.*

At sixteen Bernice found herself pregnant and dropped out of school.

> *At the time when I dropped out of school, I was thinking about him. When I made that big change in my life, I was fully focused on him. I had not thought about my dreams, I just wanted to be with him, and if I wasn't waiting for him to come over, he wouldn't come, he would punish me. He knew that I would want to see him, and he wouldn't come see me or call me or talk to me if I had other things to do. When I dropped out of school I was fully focused on him. He came to see me more, he paid me more attention. I gave up me and I got more him, which was a good trade to me at that time.*

The pregnancy, however, resulted in a miscarriage. The next year Bernice was kicked out of her home during a quarrel about her mother's drinking and her relationship with Billy. Bernice moved in with Billy. Another miscarriage occurred, probably owing to stress and physical attacks, for the relationship had become increasingly violent.

> *At that time, Billy and his family offered me a haven from having to deal with all my problems at home. I didn't want to work. I just wanted to be a housewife and have children and not be responsible for my own life. Although my mother's relationships hadn't worked out well, and even though I was doing the same thing as she did, I didn't expect the same outcome. I was going to show them how to do this.*

In the beginning Billy would slap Bernice or grab her arm or wrist. At the time she thought that this was his method of showing affection, his

way of saying that he didn't want to be without her. Bernice thought
that "this was not a big problem that was going to grow to become a
major problem."

> Billy would say, "I don't want you to go out with that girlfriend. I
> want you to stay here with me, because I miss you when you are
> gone." When he first started to say these things to me, it felt good.
> Oh, somebody wants me, wants my attention. So I would cancel the
> date with my friend. It was that attention, and I wanted it. But
> when that wore off and I would say, "I want to see my friend and I
> can see you later," Billy would get physical. And to prevent the
> violence, I would give in. I felt like a little person. I wanted to hide.
> I didn't know how to fight or deal with what was happening to me.

Bernice knew that Billy's control and abuse were becoming major problems, but for a variety of reasons she was unable to fight it. Bernice says
it took her many years to finally accept the fact that Billy was an abuser,
pure and simple.

> When he started abusing me, I would do like any other person
> involved in domestic violence does. I would say, that is a one-time
> thing, he did that because I didn't cook, or I did stay up too late
> outside on the porch. I would say to myself, I'm making him un-
> happy, it's what I'm doing, it's what I'm wearing, it's how I look.

Bernice also wanted people to see her and Billy as the perfect couple.
She couldn't live with the fact that she had escaped from one dysfunctional violent world into another. Now Bernice realizes that, when all
was said and done, her being with Billy was more important than his
abusing her. "My need for him was much bigger than him abusing
me."

When Bernice was eighteen she made up her mind to leave Billy.
Her decision to leave caused her first severe beating. At the time, Bernice was again pregnant, and she suffered another miscarriage.

> I guess I had made a partial decision that maybe I should try this
> relationship thing with someone else, so I could do a comparison. I
> did leave Billy. But the beatings then got so rough that I gave in. I

*said to myself, this isn't a situation I can just walk away from. I
began to think of Billy as a person who would take my life. I realized
this was serious.*

I ask Bernice why she didn't go ahead and get a job as a means to escape
her violent situation. Bernice says the only job she could have gotten
was at an entry level. "I should fight for my life just to get to Burger
King? I don't think so. At the time, it didn't seem to be worth dying
over."

Today Bernice has been thinking a lot about her adolescent self. She
marvels at her powerlessness. The word that Bernice uses over and over
to describe her teen years is "confusion." Her relationship, with its
mixture of obsessive romance and violence, thoroughly mixed her up.
Bernice's own dependence on Billy and the relationship, when she
knew it was slowly obliterating her own individuality, was "totally
puzzling."

> *I was very confused. It seemed like to me somehow there should be
> more, but yet I wasn't getting more. Not everybody seemed like they
> were as unhappy as I was. I didn't understand, if this was a normal
> thing, why was I so unhappy.*
>
> *The relationship wasn't making me happy. I loved him very
> much. The rest of it wasn't making me happy. I felt like there was
> no more life, this was the way I was going to live, this was it, the
> ultimate, my peak. I felt like these roles were going on, it was a
> play, and we were playing these roles. If you fought against the role,
> that is when you would get beaten.*
>
> *I could look outside myself and see me playing this role. I felt
> like I wasn't existing. Every year that went on, I felt like I was
> giving me up, that I didn't exist in this life and this world.*

The work of researchers who have sought to understand women's development through the lens of their relationships with men can shed
some light on Bernice's confusion. Some of their work focuses especially on African American women on welfare as does this book, not
only because of Bernice's story, but also because blacks now outnumber
whites on the welfare rolls, as white women are leaving welfare much

faster than women of color. Black and Hispanic women on welfare outnumbered whites by about two to one in 1998.[2]

The sociologist Beth Richie has analyzed why some African American women land—and stay—in abusive relationships. As a result of her research with thirty-seven women, mostly victims of domestic violence, at the Rose M. Singer Center at Rikers Island Correctional Facility in New York City, Richie found that for the women, whose lives were characterized by extreme poverty or sexual abuse and violence, ideologically normal families were considered a potential way out of their despair. "Their yearning and efforts to attain structurally traditional families were important initial elements of gender entrapment."[3] African American women who were not battered, she found, were not seeking or did not place as much emphasis on creating a household structurally different from the ones in which they grew up. These women did not invest as much energy into establishing long-term, monogamous relationships with men, preferring more episodic romantic relationships.

For the African American battered woman in Richie's study, a woman on her own was almost by definition a poor woman, an unsuccessful woman, and a bad mother. These women's interests in fitting in, in creating nuclear families, and in trying to make them "work" against all odds drain them "emotionally, physically, and materially." The onset of physical and emotional abuse so deeply contradicted the women's expectations that they initially deny the seriousness and rationalize the abuse, ultimately finding themselves isolated and in very dangerous situations.[4]

The newspaper columnist Jill Nelson also characterizes the particular bind of poor African American women:

> We superimpose the construct of the typical American family, à la "Leave It to Beaver" and "The Brady Bunch," over our very different lives and, like the wicked stepsisters and that shoe in Cinderella, try and make it fit. We may be bloodied, hobbling, and in excruciating economic, political, and psychic pain, but we're determined to go to the ball. As partners we mimic the idealized rituals and structure of the patriarchal, nuclear family, deny that it is a terrible design and fit, and refuse to go about the crucial business of creat-

ing workable, alternative structures, ones that take into account economic reality, social needs, and the statistical
unavailability of black men. In our communities we have
forgotten the interwoven sense of individual and collective
responsibility that helped us survive, succeed, and excel
prior to integration. [5]

Bernice's yearning for a proper nuclear family was the motivation that
propelled her into her serious relationship with Billy, causing her to
close her eyes to and ignore the ever-menacing indications that the
situation was leading her into a dangerous trap. Indeed, Bernice's en-
snarement in violence illustrates the strength and proves the validity of
Richie's theory.

In a different approach, Mary Field Belenky and her colleagues
make the linkage for us between speechlessness and violence. In families where at least one parent routinely uses violence rather than words
for influencing others' behaviors, children grow up without opportunities for play and dialogue. "Exterior dialogues are a necessary precursor
to inner speech and an awareness of one's own thought process. . . .
Without playing, conversing, listening to others, and drawing out their
own voice, people fail to develop a sense that they can talk and think
things through." Thus outer speech is important for the development
of inner speech and the sense of mind. "Feeling cut off from all internal
and external sources of intelligence, the women fail to develop their
minds and see themselves as remarkably powerless and dependent on
others for survival." Moreover, the authors found that these silent
women, who had grown up in families in which discussion was discouraged, were brought up to think that they should keep their troubles
to themselves, further increasing their isolation.[6]

Women, say the authors, see themselves as deaf and dumb when
"raised in profound isolation under the most demeaning circumstances,
not because of their genetic intellectual endowment. That anyone
emerges from their childhood years with so little confidence in their
meaning-making and their meaning-sharing abilities . . . signals the
failure of the community to receive all of those entrusted into its care."[7]

The authors further delineate the terrible effects of violence on children's intellectual development. The ever-present fear of violence prevents children from developing capabilities for hearing and knowing.

"Children develop their intellectual capacities for finding order in the world only if they have some basis for trusting that order does, indeed, exist." Because of its unpredictable nature, violence interferes with this necessary sense of an ordered world, essential for the development of healthy children.[8]

Applying this line of thought to Bernice's situation produces new insights. Raised in a violent home by parents incapable of expressing themselves verbally, Bernice herself became a silent woman who failed to develop the thought processes necessary for independent living or survival. Recently I listened to a tape Bernice made of her own interviews with her mother, her mother's ex-husband, and her sister, Brenda, about which Bernice was excited. For me the tape was thoroughly disappointing. There were no insights from Bernice's relatives; most of them came from Bernice herself, reliving her teen years and reminding her parents about what had happened. What is obvious to the listener is that Bernice's mother and stepfather have no speech. On the tape they have to be coaxed to come forward with any views, and they seem incapable of much abstract thought.

The problem with this theory is that it depicts many girls and women like Bernice as extremely passive persons, seeking to define or identify themselves solely in terms of relationships. Lyn Mikel Brown and Carol Gilligan posit a slightly different paradigm, which views girls in their adolescent years to be in conflict between their own individuality and what they know to be true about the relationships into which they are moving. Brown and Gilligan speak continually of the sense of confusion and loss that girls experience during their adolescent years as they undergo this struggle.

> Girls at the edge of adolescence face a central relational crisis: to speak what they know through experience of themselves and of relationships creates political problems—disagreement with authorities, disrupting relationships—while not to speak leaves a residue of psychological problems: false relationships and confusion as to what they feel and think.[9]

Like the girl Liza, whose story is told in their book, Bernice "no longer knows how she feels and what her point of view is, and so she is persuaded in the name of love to remain in an emotionally abusive relationship." Overcome by her boyfriend's romantic sacrifices and

hurt feelings, Liza justifies staying in a possessive and oppressive relationship by coming to believe that her desire to have her own freedom
is "irrational." Ultimately, the relationships cause not only confusion
but also a kind of moral crisis for the girls that can be paralyzing.

No one explanation may contain all of the truth, but the strength
of the Brown and Gilligan model is its presentation of a more dynamic
picture of girls who do try to resist losing their voice and identity. As
we shall soon see, Bernice's story reflects this kind of resistance.

꽃

The violence grew worse and worse as Billy used it to enforce his efforts
at control.

> I wasn't allowed to be outside my apartment, to be in a training
> program, or to have a job, or to go to school. My life was inside that
> apartment. I couldn't go to the grocery store by myself. I couldn't go
> to the Laundromat; I couldn't go over to a friend's house. I couldn't
> have people at my house. I could only talk with my family on the
> telephone. I couldn't wear certain clothes. I couldn't go to church.
>
> I had to stay home while he was at work. He would call to
> make sure that I was home. I would watch TV and read a lot. He
> wouldn't bother me with my books, as long as I wasn't spending
> time away from the house. If Billy was feeling really insecure, he
> would not only call, but he would also come home to check. It finally
> got to the point that he knew that I had so much fear that he didn't
> have to call anymore, he knew I was there.
>
> I never had company at the house. When I would go to the
> welfare office he would go with me and sit outside in the car. He
> would go with me to the doctor. If I had to go to the hospital or the
> WIC office, he would take me.
>
> Billy was totally against leaving the children with a babysitter
> and didn't approve of any day care centers. Summer camp also repre-
> sented too much outside interference. He said that children got sexu-
> ally abused in day care centers or summer camp, and the next thing
> you would know, the Department of Children and Family Services
> would take your babies from you because they would say you were
> unfit. They were all rationales for isolating the children and me. He
> would always work to keep all the outside world away.

As Billy intended, Bernice was restrained by terror.

> My fear level was so high. That was what controlled me. He con-
> trolled me through fear. When I disobeyed him, I would get beaten.
> I lived in a state of fear for over ten years. My whole day was filled
> with, what is he going to do to me today? The time seemed to go by
> that way. My whole life was passing me by. After a while, Billy no
> longer had to isolate me. I isolated myself. I slept an incredible
> number of hours. Mentally I was drained. Sluggish. I overate. I
> isolated myself.
>
> I wanted out, but I wasn't going anywhere because of my fear.
> With each incident the trap door was closing tighter. I could not see
> my way out of it. I saw myself dead if I ever left the relationship.

Furthermore, Bernice says, she had nowhere to go. She had rarely been
out of her neighborhood. Never had she any money in her pocket to
do anything. And when she was just about to break out, Billy would
bring up the earlier rape by the older man in the park.

> I didn't realize that he was using that episode to control or scare me.
> I was afraid to get on the bus. I would never go outside the neighbor-
> hood. I didn't make new friends. My life did not extend outside this
> circle, and I wasn't going to try to step outside the circle, because
> every time I did, I would get hurt.

Recently Bernice asked her sister, Brenda, why she didn't try to intervene to help her at this time. Although Brenda knew about a few of the
violent episodes, she says she thought these occurred only when Bernice was trying to leave the relationship, and she assumed that when
Billy and Bernice were together everything was fine. I asked Bernice
why her family members seemed to have been in such a state of denial.
Bernice admitted that she tried to keep the domestic violence from her
family, but agreed they had seen enough to understand what was going
on with Billy. According to Bernice, more critical to her family's nonin-
terference was the fact that whenever she temporarily escaped to her
mother's place, Billy would go over there and punch out all the windows, kick the door down, and threaten her mother and father with
further violence.

22   As time went on Bernice became more entrapped in the violent
relationship. Because of her living in a state of fear,

> *when somebody would talk to me and ask me to do things I couldn't*
> *hear them. I lived inside myself and life was passing me by. I was*
> *removing myself from reality. I would look at the clock and it would*
> *be nine o'clock and then it only seemed to me that it was a few*
> *minutes later, and it would be twelve. I couldn't understand why*
> *time escaped me so much. I couldn't keep up with where my time*
> *lapses were. I would look at the clock at two o'clock and the next*
> *thing I knew it was four o'clock. I never knew where that time went.*

Bernice now understands that this phenomenon was dissociation, a
coping mechanism used by victims to reduce the stress while living
with violence. Likewise, other victims have described how they were
able to float near the ceiling or take imaginary walks during violent
episodes, or have actually induced self-hypnotic anesthesia experiences.
Experts find that this dissociative behavior often continues after the violence has ceased and interferes with the survivor's ability to function
long afterward.

> *You live inside your own world and your own mind. You can't deal*
> *with reality. People can't penetrate it, can't get through to it, because*
> *you're afraid that if you come to reality, it is going to hurt. It's like*
> *a cloud. It protects you when he is coming at you, calling you names,*
> *or when he's getting physically violent with you. It's like you can*
> *take yourself out of yourself.*

Billy introduced Bernice to marijuana at the age of sixteen.

> *He never used it much but was always trying to find something to*
> *make me happy. By twenty I was lacing the marijuana with cocaine.*
> *It numbed me. The day went by faster for me. I could get through*
> *the whole day without having a fight. When I became more depen-*
> *dent on it, then the abuse started more. He was the one that brought*
> *it home. I couldn't go out and buy it because he never really let me*
> *have any money. There was less fighting because I had to do what he*
> *wanted so I could get my drugs. What eventually helped me to stop*

*using was being able to accept my days. I wanted night to be day
and day to be night because there was nothing in that day for me.*

Beth Richie finds Bernice's experience with an ever-escalating spiral of
violence not atypical. In her research she traces the trajectory of the
violence and the African American woman's reactions to it. Because of
the profound importance of the partnerships and the high expectations
women had of them, Richie reports that at first there was disbelief and
a hope that the violence would stop without severing the relationships.
Wanting to hide the shame of a public failure, the women worked hard
to conceal the situation from others. "The African American battered
women's failure to successfully create safer households represented a
serious challenge to their identities and sense of competence in the
private sphere, and as their efforts to help themselves failed, the violence got worse. Ultimately, they found themselves isolated and in very
dangerous situations, vulnerable to extreme forms of abuse."[10]

Nor is this denial limited to African American women. Many
women who have invested heavily in their intimate relationships will
be slow to admit to themselves that the reality is less than perfect. Listen
to the British actress Alex Kingston reflecting upon her relatively long
marriage to screen and stage star Ralph Fiennes, from whom she is now
divorced: "As a woman, you are conditioned into thinking that your
marriage, your great love, is going to be this fairy-tale existence. Even
if it's not, you try and make it so. Women are very good at doing this,
even though ultimately they may be desperately unhappy."[11]

As compelling and interesting as Bernice's story of entrapment is, how
typical is it? How many Bernices are out there? The sobering answer is
many. For the last several years welfare-to-work programs providing
intensive and long-term assistance to women on welfare have discovered that many women on welfare are current domestic violence victims. Although we had long understood that many women escaping
domestic violence apply for welfare and have used its benefits as a crucial ingredient in their escape planning, we had not realized that many
women already on welfare become involved in intimate relationships
that are violent. Women on welfare, it is easy to assume, are unmarried,
single mothers raising their children without a man in their lives, and

24   as a result we have not thought to consider a different reality. Because
single motherhood was a prerequisite for eligibility for the welfare program, women went to great lengths to keep the existence of their relationships with men hidden.

Only when many states implemented new welfare plans, made possible by federal waivers, that required recipients to work did welfare
department staffs and welfare-to-work programs become aware of the
issue of domestic violence. Bill Curcio, a welfare department official in
Passaic County, New Jersey, relates his awakening to the issue of domestic violence:

> I had already worked for the welfare department for twenty-
> two years. And when I took over the Life Skills Program, I
> thought I knew what was really happening out there. Having
> come up through the ranks in the welfare department, I
> thought I understood the dynamics of poverty. And that
> soon changed. . . . During the self-exploration phase of Life
> Skills, which lasts from about five to seven days, we go
> through a number of exercises to get the students to think
> about how they got to this point. They take stock of their
> lives, in essence, so they can move on from there. While I
> was teaching this class on Self-Exploration, stories of domes-
> tic abuse and sexual trauma kept coming up over and over
> again in the class. And everyone was deeply engaged in the
> discourse about these issues. Many of the students would ask
> to speak to the trainers privately after class if they weren't
> strong enough to really talk about it openly in class.
>
> And so this was a part of welfare that I had never seen
> before. . . . I began to see over and over again horrible stories
> and a huge number of these stories. Simultaneously I was
> observing overt manifestations of this whole issue. People
> would come to class beat up, with black eyes, or they would
> disappear from class for a couple of days. And stalking. We'd
> have to call the police a number of times. The very first time
> I taught the class, a person went out for a break. I never saw
> her again. I found out days later that when she went outside
> the building to smoke a cigarette, her boyfriend grabbed
> her, threw her in the car, whisked her away, and she was

gone. So the combination of the stories in class, what was being physically manifested, and the fact that students would ask to speak to me personally, I was being educated to something I didn't even know was going on.[12]

A fair number of welfare-to-work programs tracking the issue found that well over half their participants were current domestic violence victims.[13] Because these programs contain mixes of mandatory and voluntary participants, it was until recently impossible to say with any certainty what the prevalence of domestic violence was for the entire welfare caseload. By reason of their more rigorous methodologies, eight relatively new research studies allow us to add quantitative data to these anecdotes. The numbers are relatively high and consistent across all studies. Because battered women are reluctant to admit to domestic violence, researchers caution that the prevalence of domestic violence reported in research studies is bound to be an underrepresentation of the true prevalence.

National surveys estimate that domestic violence is a factor in approximately 6 percent of all U.S. households.[14] During the past five years researchers have consistently found that 20 to 30 percent of women receiving welfare benefits are current victims of domestic violence, and approximately two-thirds are former victims. With approximately two million women on welfare during fiscal year 1998 (October 1997–September 1998), as many as 400,000 women could be affected nationwide.[15]

Bill Curcio developed a sample of 846 women on welfare, all mandatory participants in education, training, and jobs-related activities between December 1995 and January 1997 in Passaic County, New Jersey. These participants were confidentially surveyed during the course of an eight-week life skills program at a time when they had been in the program for over a week, when security and mutual support had been established, and when participants had already shared their life experiences with the class. Curcio cautions that respondents in this sample are those who showed up and remained in the program for the first two weeks. Those who didn't come or dropped out are probably those women with the most problems of one kind or another, and it can be assumed that a number of them are domestic violence victims prohibited from attending. Curcio's study found that approximately 15 percent of the entire sample were current victims of domestic violence, defined as physical violence. An additional 25 percent reported current verbal or emotional abuse.[16]

The University of Massachusetts Boston Center for Survey Research designed a survey representing the first scientific sampling of one state's entire welfare caseload that measures both current and past prevalence of domestic violence. Seven hundred and thirty-four women, a representative sample of women on welfare in the state, were confidentially interviewed in all welfare department offices throughout Massachusetts between January and June 1996. Using the definition of domestic violence in the Massachusetts Abuse Prevention Act, the study found 19.5 percent of the entire sample reporting physical violence at the hands of an intimate partner within the previous twelve months.[17]

Susan Lloyd, a researcher affiliated with the Northwestern University/University of Chicago Joint Center for Poverty Research, conducted a random survey of 824 women in one low-income neighborhood in Chicago, Illinois. Between September 1994 and May 1995 Lloyd's researchers randomly selected and screened the women in both English and Spanish in their homes for approximately fifty-five minutes. Lloyd's study enables us to compare the prevalence of domestic violence within the smaller sample of those women on welfare to the entire sample as a whole.

Although the study does not find any appreciable differences in the rates of violence among women differentiated by race or ethnicity, women in the lowest income levels, including those on welfare, experienced all forms of abuse at higher levels than the women in the highest income group. When incidence of physical aggression over the last twelve months was measured, women on welfare had experienced nearly three times the amount of violence experienced by nonwelfare women in the neighborhood (31 percent compared to almost 12 percent). Using a definition measuring more severe aggression within the past twelve months, which includes rape or threatening with or using a weapon, almost 12 percent of the entire sample had been so abused, compared with almost 20 percent of the welfare sample.[18]

Two other studies also found a higher prevalence of domestic violence within households of women on welfare. In a survey of one thousand women residing in the state of Utah during April and May 1997, one in five respondents claimed that their children currently witness or hear verbal abuse, while one in fourteen stated that their children witness or hear physical abuse. Utah women who qualify for welfare had a greater tendency to say that their children hear or witness physical abuse: about 28 percent of welfare-eligible women, compared to 7 percent of noneligible women. In addition, welfare qualifiers were more inclined to report being victims of isolation (defined as someone controlling what others do and to whom they talk; limiting outside involvement; and using jealousy to justify actions). About four in ten (41 percent) of welfare-eligible women said they experience some isolation, compared to 11 percent of noneligible women.

Moreover, welfare qualifiers were more inclined than the average respondent to have obtained a civil protective order and to have dealt with the courts regarding domestic violence situations. Twenty-eight percent of welfare-eligible women said yes, compared to 7 percent of noneligible women, to a question of whether they had ever obtained a civil protective order. Roughly the same percentages stated that they had ever dealt with the courts as a result of domestic violence situations.[19]

In 1993 the Commonwealth Fund's Survey on Women's Health undertook a national telephone survey of more than two thousand women over the age of eighteen. Researchers asked whether certain behaviors occurred within the last five years with the partner with whom the respondent was currently living. Although 24 percent of the women on welfare reported domestic violence in the past five years with their current partner, only 7 percent of other respondents reported domestic violence.[20]

Similar and equally sobering statistics come from the Worcester Family Research Project, a five-year study of 436 women, most of whom were welfare recipients, both homeless and housed in Worcester, Massachusetts, conducted by the Better Homes Fund between August 1992 and July 1995. Respondents took part in three to four face-to-face interview sessions lasting over ten hours. The Worcester Study found that nearly one-third of the women had experienced severe violence from their current or most recent partner within the last two years. One-third reported that an intimate partner had threatened to kill them. Moreover, about two-thirds had experienced severe physical assault by a parent or other caretaker while growing up, and over 40 percent had been sexually molested before reaching adulthood.[21]

28   Fascinating data illuminating the relationship of violence and welfare usage is also a part of the Worcester study. A fluid pattern of welfare use among study respondents became apparent, with approximately one-third of the sample reporting more than one stay on welfare. These women cycle on and off welfare ("cyclers"), and were three times more likely to have worked in the past year than were continuous welfare users. Interestingly, the study found that with all their cycling on and off welfare, these women used welfare for longer total durations than those who stayed on continuously. Cyclers, however, were more likely to have experienced violence than were continuous users. Rates of violent victimization, both in childhood and adulthood, high across the sample, were uniformly higher in the long-term welfare group for all types of victimization.[22]

In a recent study involving a random sample of 753 women on welfare in a medium-size city in Michigan undertaken by the University of Michigan Research Development Center on Poverty, Risk, and Mental Health, when defining physical abuse as either moderate physical violence or severe violence, nearly a quarter (23 percent) of the women in the sample experienced physical abuse in the past twelve months, and 63 percent encountered abuse in their lifetime in intimate relationships.[23]

In 1997 Lisa Brush of the University of Pittsburgh interviewed 122 incoming enrollees at six sites of the briefest welfare-to-work program serving those participants deemed job-ready by the county. Thirty-eight percent of that sample disclosed physical violence or injury in their current or most recent relationship; 27 percent of the sample were seriously physically abused, and over two-thirds (almost 69 percent) reported domestic violence ever in their lives.[24] And, in a random sample of 325 women on welfare in Utah, 12 percent had experienced domestic violence within the previous twelve months.[25]

Although differing definitions of domestic violence were employed in the research, the emerging data are remarkably consistent. It would appear that at least 20 to 30 percent of women on welfare are current domestic violence victims, meaning that the number of women like Bernice, trapped by poverty and abuse, is quite high. Bernice's experiences in trying to work in order to get off welfare, to which we will now turn, thus have much to tell us about what welfare reform needs to look like for a considerable part of the welfare population.

CHAPTER TWO

Trying to Work

> Intellectual freedom depends upon material things. Poetry
> depends upon intellectual freedom. And women have
> always been poor, not for two hundred years merely, but
> from the beginning of time. Women have had less
> intellectual freedom than the sons of Athenian slaves.
> Women, then, have not had a dog's chance of writing
> poetry. That is why I have laid so much stress on money and
> a room of one's own.
>
> —VIRGINIA WOOLF, *A Room of One's Own*

Bernice was trapped not only by her desires for a nuclear family of her own but also by her welfare receipt. She spent a total of eight years on welfare, all of them when she was living with Billy and trapped by violence. Eventually Bernice applied for welfare because Billy wouldn't let her work, but he wasn't employed enough on a regular basis to support the family.

Billy would go from one factory job to another at minimum wage. Work for Billy was a revolving door, and the result was long stretches of unemployment. Today Bernice thinks that Billy used to get himself fired because he wanted to be at home, watching Bernice.

> *He was happier at home. He would stay at home with me. Every-*
> *thing I would do within my day, he would do too. He watched the*

*soap operas, he would do the laundry, we would go to the grocery
store. We did everything together.*

Bernice says Billy was also grateful to have the welfare check and encouraged her application. Because he was frequently out of work, there
was never enough cash to keep all the bills current. Although her welfare check was $368 a month, Bernice's rent was $500 a month. As a
result, Bernice says, she paid the rent in cash and food stamps. After
that, she would sell some more of the stamps for cash and make what
food she had stretch until the end of the month. Bernice's parents gave
her extra pocket money, twenty dollars here and there, which enabled
her to just get by.

Like many battered women, Bernice tried many times over the
years to escape welfare for work, both as a means of eliminating the
violence as well as having the economic wherewithal to make a better
life for herself and her children. At every turn Billy sabotaged her efforts.

As a prelude to getting a good job, at age nineteen, Bernice decided to go back to school to get her high school equivalency (GED) certificate.

> *I was going to school at night and he was working during the day.
> He didn't want me to go to night school. He would come home and
> say, "I can't take you to school tonight because I am too tired
> today," so I would tell him, "Okay, just get out of the way, I'll
> catch the bus and go." We fought all the way to school and all the
> way back home. Night school was only three nights a week, but we
> fought. Physically. We would fight outside the school. He would take
> my coat in the winter, hide my coat from me, because he felt by me
> saying that it was time for me to get up and do something with my
> life, he did not want me to get up and meet new people and feel that
> I was achieving something.*

Bernice loved night school. The teachers were great, the classes were
small, and she enjoyed learning new skills. "But I had to fight with my
life to get there." When she failed the GED test the first time around by
two points, Bernice says, Billy said, "See, I told you, you weren't going

to do it no way." But Bernie just had to have her GED. "My ambition triggered the terrible whipping I then received over the GED test."

Billy became very aggressive after Bernice got her GED. Bernice decided that, since she and Billy were already fighting, they "might as well fight about something important," so she registered for a training course to become a medical assistant. Part of the program involved a thirty-day internship at a local hospital. On the evening of the twenty-ninth day Billy grabbed Bernice, tied her up, beat her, and raped her. At work the next day Bernice's swollen face and bruises garnered a great deal of attention, and the staff did not want her to be in front of the patients. Throughout the day Bernice's supervisor followed her around, watching what she was doing. Although she completed the internship, the hospital did not offer Bernice a position. Much later Bernice found out that her supervisor had given her a poor report that prevented her from obtaining a job with another employer.

❧

Welfare-to-work and job training providers around the country report similar stories of education- and work-related sabotage. Women's partners tear up books and homework assignments, rip clothing and winter coats, and inflict visible bruises to prevent the women from attending class. Promising to drive the women to classes or work, their partners consistently bring them late in the hopes that they will be dismissed. One abuser shaved off all his partner's hair in order to embarrass her.[1] Karen Brown, formerly of the City Works job training program in the Bronx, wrote me about some of these practices:

> On a much more general level, [abuse takes the form of] the withholding of support for the student when she would need it most—before a crucial second interview, GED test, etc. Often students will get into altercations with their partners before such crucial events, causing them either to miss the event altogether or arrive in such an agitated state that their performance is compromised. After this became a pattern I personally began to suspect that it was not a coincidence that these events were occurring right before the important job-related event that was important for the student.[2]

32　At the Chicago Commons Employment Training Center I met a woman whose arm was in a cast. The night before her GED practice test her partner engineered an argument and broke her right arm. (She is right-handed.) When the same action occurred the second time before the scheduled GED practice test, she realized it for the deliberate sabotage it was. The GED test appears to constitute a considerable provocation to abusers and figures in many an anecdote. Molly Robertson, the administrator of the "GED on TV" program in Indiana, reports that she gets telephone calls from many students who tell her that their husbands or boyfriends have thrown away their GED study books. Although a formal study has not yet been undertaken, Ms. Robertson believes that research would reveal that those women who do not continue to pursue the GED certificate are those whose partners are nonsupportive and abuse them.[3]

Anecdotes shared by the women and their welfare-to-work counselors across the country reflect the considerable ingenuity of the abusers. One former welfare participant, for example, telephoned me to say that she had been unsuccessfully applying for a job over a two-year period. Eventually she noticed she was being trailed by a particular van. When the license plate was checked she discovered that it was a surveillance company hired by her former boyfriend. He would then call potential employers and say whatever it would take to make certain that she would not be hired. Only when she was able to halt this practice was she able to land a job.

Sylvia Benson of STRIVE/Chicago Job Service told me of a woman she sent out for an interview for a very good job in the suburbs. When she did not show up for the interview, Benson contacted her. She was told that the woman's partner had agreed to drive her to the interview. "He was not quite happy that she was going to be working or even trying to get out and find employment for herself. They started arguing and one thing led to another and he started hitting her. So by the time she did get out there she was beaten up." After the beating her partner turned the car around, dumping her off on the side of the road halfway back. The badly bruised woman had to hitchhike home.

Benson also described the case of another client, a recovering heroin addict, whose abuser interferes with her staying off drugs. "She said to me the other day, 'You know, I think he likes the fact that I use drugs because he knows I won't go anywhere. He has even supplied me to keep me from leaving.' My client is now on her third try at getting clean." Still another woman was helped by STRIVE to find a job at the front desk of a major company. Because her partner kept coming around, she would continually leave her station to shoo him out, trying to calm him down in the parking lot. Noticing her absences, her employer reprimanded her. Although the employee explained the situation, she received no support from her employer and was fired three days later.[4]

Another case manager at a welfare-to-work program told me of a woman on methadone maintenance who is waiting for a slot at a federally funded drug program. Since her state Medicaid program doesn't cover this drug, she has to buy the methadone herself. When she enrolled in a GED program against the will of her partner, he withheld the funds so she could not buy her needed methadone. Not surprisingly, the woman subsequently dropped out of the program.

Nor is kidnapping from job training programs unknown. Carol, a participant in a GED class, told me she was secretly attending class, going to school on the bus and returning home before her partner did. "I am determined to get my GED. The only way I won't get it is if he kidnaps me and takes me. He's done it before." Corinna landed a job she loved at a local elementary school. Her partner constantly accused her of having an affair with the bus driver and beat her so viciously over it that Corinna had to quit the job and go back on welfare.[5]

From a domestic violence demonstration project in one of the welfare offices in San Antonio, Texas, come these stories:

> I was working. I was getting up in my life. I [was] becoming what I wanted to be. I liked my job. I was doing good—It was a convenience store, and he didn't like it that much, because there were a lot of men coming in. I mean it was a convenience store; they would stop for gas. He would stalk me outside. He would be watching me. He was across the street, and he parked his car, and he would be watching me, and if a guy would stay too long at the counter, God knows, [he thought] I would have slept with him. . . . And my bills got really out of control, and he damaged the house really bad.

34   Another woman relates:

> There were times where I couldn't even get out of my room
> because I still had a handprint on my face. I couldn't go to
> work because it was embarrassing—going to work, and you
> know that you are terrified. Or going to work and saying
> that you really don't want to go home, and not being able
> to say why I don't want to go home.[6]

Jocelyn, who weighed 390 pounds when she started at a welfare-to-
work program, told me that she believed her partner wanted her fat
and kept her that way by encouraging her eating. Clearly, she was un-
employable at that weight. Once she entered the program, Jocelyn lost
over one hundred pounds.[7]

Another common ploy is the use of false statements and accusations. As soon as Anita was promoted from cashier to assistant manager,
her partner drove to work and told the manager that he was deathly ill
and Anita had to quit work to take care of him. Then he physically
dragged her away. Several months before, he had bodily removed Anita
from the computer course she was taking.[8]

False accusations can make life hard for battered women. To keep
them in line their abusers often threaten to call the welfare department
to report their own illegal presence and financial support in the wom-
en's lives. From a Kansas City, Missouri, focus group study comes an
appalling example of this tactic. Separated from her abuser, a mother of
one was enrolled in a paralegal training program. To retaliate against
her, he called the state's child protective service to complain that she
was abusing her daughter.

> I made an appointment to meet the worker so he could
> come to investigate us for eight o'clock Monday morning
> because I had to get to school. And that Sunday night he
> came and we had a horrible assault situation. I'm pressing
> charges at four o'clock in the morning at the police station,
> and before that I had to take my daughter to my mother's
> house because I don't want her to go to the police station. I
> didn't even have time to go to the emergency room until
> the next afternoon because I had to meet the worker at eight

o'clock in the morning and then go to school. This abuse causes me to miss school all the time and I couldn't tell all these people, so I had to come up with reasons as to why. And now I think, I can't believe that I was assaulted and I remember being grateful that it was just my body and not my face, I didn't have any bruises. With the police station, the eight o'clock thing and then school, I couldn't even go to the emergency room.[9]

Recently I heard about another example of this kind of partner sabotage. After his partner separated herself from him, obtained a restraining order, and sued for child support, the abuser approached the welfare department, telling the authorities that his partner had received welfare illegally because he had been in the household the entire time. The welfare department is now trying to collect forty-one thousand dollars from the mother of three, who is now working and off welfare, even though the woman has testified that while he was in the home her partner, a crack addict, consistently commandeered the welfare check for his own uses.[10]

Sabotage of child care arrangements is also common. Women report that for an important job interview their abusers promise to watch the children but either fail to show up, appear inebriated, or leave the children at home unattended. One woman in the Kansas City focus group reported that because her ex-partner kept kidnapping her children, she was afraid to leave them in a child care center during the day.[11] The University of Massachusetts Boston caseload survey found that almost 24 percent of the abused women surveyed (compared to 9 percent of the nonabused) had argued over visitation within the last year, and almost 15 percent of the abused (compared to about 5 percent of the never abused) had had disputes over child custody within the last twelve months. Not surprisingly, fears for children's safety and whereabouts can make employment outside the home difficult.[12]

In May 1997 the Virginia Department of Social Services asked its local departments whether they had encountered clients who may have had difficulty in meeting work requirements because of domestic violence. Caseworkers responded with some typical scenarios. One recalled a client held hostage for a day because her boyfriend didn't want her to come to Stepping Stones (the welfare department's pre-employment

36   program). The woman's partner also later stole her car so that she couldn't get to the job skills training program. A former abusing boyfriend was stalking another. She had a restraining order, but was fearful of being outside her home and had difficulty following through with welfare-to-work assignments. In another case an ex-boyfriend called the telephone company and had the woman's telephone disconnected so that it was harder for her to contact the employer that sent her out on temporary jobs. The complexity of the domestic violence issue is illustrated by this submission from another caseworker:

> "I can't lie about this anymore. The reason I am not at school is because my boyfriend hit me last night and I have a huge bruise on the side of my face. I don't want anyone to see me like this." This is why she was always gone. No matter what I said to her she was not fulfilling her work requirement and her school attendance was the pits. Finally I knew what was going on and could help her start addressing it. I gave her all the numbers, talked to her about the dynamics of abuse, told her what the police could do, and she seemed receptive. Three days later she was back at school. She called the numbers, got more information and told him to leave her alone. She was sure he would. Two weeks later we were back to square one, he was back again. The police arrested him for assault and battery two days later. Another three days off school. This time she was positive he would go away. He didn't and the third time she fought back and cut him with a razor blade. Fortunately, no one was seriously hurt. This is my client's life and try as I might to get her help, I can't force her. She wants out, she wants to work and succeed but she can't seem to get it together.[13]

In December 1997 Jeff Kunerth of the *Orlando Sentinel* interviewed Linda Sexton and her boyfriend, Doug Pittman, the father of Sexton's three boys. The domestic abuse accelerated when the forty-one-year-old Sexton was required to find employment under Florida's welfare reform plan. While Pittman was unemployed, Sexton worked two jobs, one as a waitress and the other as a convenience store clerk.

"I didn't want her to work," Kunerth quotes Pittman as saying. "As long as she wasn't working, I could keep her on my level." Pittman would show up at work to harass Sexton and embarrass her to try to get her fired. He broke the washing machine so she wouldn't have clean clothes to wear. He hid the car keys or disconnected the car's battery and spark plugs so she couldn't get to work. He took all her money so she didn't have bus fare. He made sure he wasn't home when she needed him to take care of the kids. "I didn't want her to succeed," Pittman said. "I didn't want her to see a better life. If she sees a better life, she'll know she doesn't need me."

In the middle of a nasty fight, to humiliate Sexton and prevent her from going to work the next day, Pittman poured red, green, and blue food coloring over her head as she sat sobbing at the kitchen table. As the police arrived, Pittman grabbed a butcher knife and sliced his left wrist two inches deep. Unable to wash the food dye from her hair, Sexton missed work. Members of her church helped her clean up the puddle of blood he left behind, and they painted her walls and shampooed the carpet.[14]

Because I had heard that domestic violence had surfaced as a problem, I spoke with a human resources officer of a major national company that had hired thirty-five to forty welfare recipients at its Chicago location. The company official confirmed that its new employees were absent, late for work, or came with visible bruises due to domestic violence, circumstances not the norm for this company. Thanks to good company security the women's partners could not penetrate into the workplace, but they harassed their partners as they got off the bus, on their way home, or on their way to child care in the evening. When I asked the official what percent appeared to be dealing with domestic violence, she replied, "All, 100 percent, on some level. It is only a matter of degree."[15]

Now quantitative research is beginning to document these anecdotes and patterns of partner sabotage of employment efforts. Current knowledge about employment for battered women on welfare presents a complex picture; it is likely that the issue will be totally unraveled only over time. In summary, most of the research results, with one important exception, present a snapshot of employment status at the time of the research or over a past period of time. The data reflect the complex pattern presented by the qualitative evidence, showing that

38   low-income battered women have many different responses to the abuse: some women struggle to work, others work but cannot sustain that employment over time because of domestic violence, and still others do not or cannot manage to work at all.

First are the studies that measure abusers' attitudes toward education, training, and employment. Bill Curcio's sample of 846 women on welfare in Passaic County, New Jersey, found that three times as many currently abused women as nonabused women stated that their intimate partner actively tried to prevent them from obtaining education or training (40 percent as compared with 13 percent for the entire sample).[16] The University of Massachusetts Boston welfare caseload sample found that abused women were ten times more likely than their never-abused counterparts to have a current or former partner who would not like their going to school or work.[17] In an assessment of 1,082 new applicants for public assistance in four Colorado welfare offices between April and December 1997, the Center for Policy Research found that 44 percent of the victims of domestic violence reported that their abusive ex-partners had prevented them from working.[18]

Women interviewed in battered women's shelters consistently reveal that their abusers did not support and often prevented their employment. In research in three domestic violence shelters in Chicago, Stephanie Riger of the University of Illinois at Chicago conducted sixty-nine in-depth interviews in 1997. Most of the women were unemployed, but almost all had worked intermittently at unskilled positions for relatively low pay. The women appeared to cycle on and off welfare, with an average over their adult lifetime of two separate times on welfare, for a total of seven years of receipt. Riger reports that just under half the women were forbidden by the abuser to get a job. Of those who worked, half of the women were fired or forced to quit their jobs as a result of the abuse. Furthermore, one-quarter of the women were forbidden to go to school by the abuser. Of those who attended school during the relationship, about one-third were forced to drop out. Common tactics employed by half the abusers included refusing to give the woman a ride, stealing her car keys or money, threatening to prevent her from leaving, harassing her in person at work or school, lying about the children's health or safety, and physically restraining her from going to work or school.[19]

A study of 372 women in twenty shelters in Ohio, as well as another undertaken by the University of Minnesota that interviewed 123 women attending domestic violence support groups, found large numbers of women admitting that their partners had discouraged or actively prevented employment. About a quarter of the Minnesota sample reported that they had lost a job partly because of being abused.[20] Interestingly, one evaluation of a teen pregnancy and parenting project found that the fact of living with a boyfriend was significantly correlated with dropping out of school. Staff members believed that male partners encourage the young women to be truant because they worry about their meeting other men in school.

Second, researchers determining employment histories over time provide a better understanding of how domestic violence can interfere with long-term workforce involvement. Susan Lloyd's neighborhood survey found that women who had suffered domestic violence in their adult relationships were more likely to have experienced spells of unemployment and to have had more job turnover, even though women who were abused were employed in roughly the same numbers as those who were not victimized at the time of the survey. Lloyd also found that respondents who reported having experienced domestic violence within the past twelve months, and who stated that their partners had directly prevented them from going to school or work or had threatened to harm their children, were less likely to be employed than women who did not experience these particular forms of abuse. Likewise, women whose partners had threatened to kill them at some point in time were less likely to be currently employed.[21]

Through her interviews with mandatory welfare-to-work participants in Pittsburgh, Lisa Brush makes some basic correlation between domestic violence and success or failure in a welfare-to-work program. Only a small minority of the 122 women were able to find a job within the twenty program days, and fourteen women (11 percent) dropped out. The vast majority (73 percent) completed the program, thus complying with the work requirements imposed by their welfare department. Through an intricate analysis Brush was able to isolate those aspects of domestic violence that she demonstrated to have a controlling effect on ability to complete the program or to find employment. She found, for example, that women who had sought an order of protection as a result of the domestic violence dropped out at six times the rate of

40   women who did not, strong evidence that battered women facing a safety crisis in the short term will be unable to comply with welfare reform requirements. However, women who reported being hit, kicked, or coerced into sex, if they worked at all, had significantly higher job placement rates than their peers whose partners did not batter or harass them in these ways. This finding confirms the results of other studies, such as Lloyd's, that concluded that some battered women try to use work as a way to escape domestic violence. Brush also discovered that those women whose intimate partners objected to their going to work because of conformity with traditional expectations about motherhood and housewifery experienced higher dropout rates (at statistically significant levels) than those whose partners did not. Women who stated that their intimate partners told them that working mothers are bad mothers dropped out five times as frequently as women not subjected to these messages.[22]

The first research that enables us to track domestic violence and employment over a five-year period is the Worcester Family Research Project. Of the 436 women in the baseline study, 356 were reinterviewed between May 1994 and November 1996, and 327 were again interviewed between September 1995 and August 1997. Researchers asked detailed questions pertaining to income, jobs, welfare usage, and domestic violence during the follow-up time periods, enabling them to correlate domestic violence with maintaining work at least thirty hours per week for six months or more. The project has recently reported on the experiences of 285 women with employment.

When women were simply asked whether they had worked at all in the past twelve months, there were no significant differences between women who were victims of domestic violence and those who were not in the past year. It was only when the level of work was defined with more specificity that the effects of partner violence emerged. Controlling for a variety of demographic, psychosocial, and health variables that were significantly associated with recent physical aggression or violence, women who experienced physical aggression during the first twelve-month follow-up period had about one-third the odds of working at least thirty hours per week for six months or more during the following year as did women who had not experienced such aggression. It was the recent (past twelve months) experiences with physical violence by male partners—rather than earlier partner violence—that

predicted reduced capacity to maintain work the subsequent year. Like
Brush's data, the Worcester Project data demonstrates that serious episodes of domestic violence within the past twelve months appeared
most likely to adversely affect women's abilities to work.[23]

⚜

For Billy, Bernice's potential employment was a continued provocation,
and he persevered in his efforts to keep Bernice away from working.

> If I work, I am going to interact with people. I am going to make
> money, develop skills. I am going to have confidence, be dedicated to
> something other than him. People will be allowed to have input. I
> will start to come alive, I will care about the way I look, the way I
> dress, and ultimately I will want something different outside of my
> current life. Billy knew that our life was nothing. If I went to work,
> he would have lost me. He knew it, and that was what he was afraid
> of. He was right. If I had been able to get a job, I would have been
> gone.

After Bernice couldn't find a job as a medical assistant because of the
bad review given her by her training program, she stayed in the house
but made sporadic and unsuccessful attempts to leave. As a result of her
numerous tries, the violence got even more serious. Billy began using
cigarettes, an iron, and a broom. He also bought a gun. Following
Bernice's return after one attempt to leave, Billy forced her to sleep in
the hallway for days as punishment. This was the pattern. Bernice might
forget her dream for a few months, but eventually she would try again.
Her struggle was the way she kept going.

The next year, Bernice decided to try to reach out again. Seeing a
leaflet at her son's school about a new welfare-to-work program in her
community, Bernice decided to attend. Billy accompanied her to the
first day of classes at the Chicago Commons Employment Training Center and, according to Bernice, tried to enroll himself as a way of monitoring her activities at the program. Only after a skirmish with the staff
did he agree to leave the scene. To continue to be able to attend the
program, Bernice had to lie about what was going on there.

*I always had to make it seem like this school was a waste of time. I
had my own little secrets, that I was achieving things, and I had
goals, short-term goals and long-term goals.*

It took many months for Bernice to share her predicament with program staff. I remember Bernice being more involved with helping others in the class than with herself. We did not know that this was the
first time in many years that Bernice was interacting with others in a
social setting. Bernice always came to the program wearing black
clothes, and dark sunglasses stayed on all day long. A black wool ski
cap always covered her hair. She seemed to have only two different
moods: anger or depression. Today, Bernice says she wore sunglasses
because she didn't want anyone to see that she was always crying.

Bernice was much more willing to speak about the behavior of her
children. Little Billy's fire-starting was an indication to her case manager
that something serious was going on in the household, so she referred
Bernice to outside counseling to sort out the situation. It took a while
for Bernice to let her therapist know what was going on.

In thinking back to that time, Bernice's therapist remembers that
Bernice was heavier. It was hard for her to see Bernice's face because
she always wore dark glasses. She saw "a distant, dark, shadowy person," but, she says, there was always a part of Bernice that was trying
to reach out. Today Bernice's therapist says that she supported her in
trying to get out of the situation safely, but that the only expert on
safety was Bernice. "She was the expert on how far you could push
Billy. I didn't know what he was capable of doing. Any therapist has to
listen to what she has to say about that, about how to be safe." She
explains that fear—Bernice's real fear for her physical safety—was the
major factor keeping Bernice where she was.

Bernice and Denise Innis, her case manager at ETC, decided that
Bernice should enroll in a one-year licensed practical nurse training
program, which would realize Bernice's longtime interest in nursing
and would greatly assist in her obtaining a well-paying job. I remember
speaking with Bernice after the program had begun. She told me that
Billy was cooperating, driving her to the classes (held in a local hospital) at six o'clock in the morning and taking care of the children's
getting to school. Elated about the training, Bernice told me that she
felt she was developing into an extremely competent nurse and wanted

to go on to become a nurse in an operating room. Now and then Billy resorted to his old tricks, however. When the weather was bad, he said he couldn't drive Benice to the hospital. Then, when she came home, he accused her of having someone else, presumably a male, pick her up. Nor did Bernice believe that she should participate in a study group, composed of both males and females, that the students had organized. The group had a useful telephone tree, and when someone ran into a problem he or she could call the others for help. Bernice knew better than to get into that telephone tree, because if a male would ever call the house, she knew she wouldn't be able to go to school the next day.

Bernice was fifteen weeks from graduation.

> I was so proud of myself. I was motivated, I had been offered a job, my life was about to change. I had one more course to go through as well as the final exam. I didn't tell Billy how close I was to gradua-tion, but unfortunately he overheard me on the telephone talking with my sister, as I was very excited to be offered a job. The weekend before the final exam he made sure we fought all weekend. He knew how important this test was for me. He wouldn't watch the children, he wouldn't feed them, he wouldn't let me study, he would take my books from me. I never got a chance to either sleep or study.

Around two o'clock Monday morning Billy raped Bernice. "When he battered and raped me, after a year of virtually no violence, it really did something to me emotionally. It paralyzed me. I said to myself, Oh my God, he is going to beat me up no matter what I do."

Exhausted and sleep-deprived, physically and mentally beaten down, Bernice dragged herself to school to take the final exam. Not surprisingly, she failed the test and was dropped from the program. Although Denise Innis, her case manager, appealed the decision to the head of the program by describing what had occurred, the school cate-gorically refused to reconsider and let Bernice retake the examination or even re-enroll in the program.

Several months later Bernice left Billy and took the children to her mother's house. Billy came there and broke all the windows in the apartment and threatened to kill Bernice's mother.

> I saw how Billy reacted when I had tried to leave in the past. I
> needed a better plan. So in the meantime, in order to protect my

mom and dad, I returned home. The fear was absolutely overwhelming.

Billy also threatened to kill Denise Innis, Bernice's case manager at ETC.

> Every time Billy would tie me up he would say, "This is what I
> am going to do to her." He was going to blow the school up, beat
> her up, cut her face, shoot her. He was going to make her have a
> car accident. All his anger was turned on Denise. He knew it con-
> trolled me.

Bernice says she felt better when Denise showed she totally refused to
be worried about Billy's threats against her.

> One day, when he made the threat again, I said, "Go ahead and kill
> her then." He pushed me down on the floor, and he put a broom
> across my neck and he had a gun in his hand and he was holding the
> broom down in the other hand and his knee was on my throat. He
> said, "You know, I could just kill you right now," and as he talked
> he moved the gun to my neck. I said, "Well, go ahead, take Denise
> out, and you might as well take me out too, and take yourself out too."
> He got up and said, "I wasn't doing anything but playing with you.
> Even if I pulled the trigger nothing would have happened." It so
> frightened me that I was still on the floor. He took the gun and put
> it in the closet and said, "You'll always know where this is at."
>   I stayed in the house for three months after that and I didn't
> get dressed. I wouldn't go out, I wouldn't feed the children. I just sat
> there in front of the TV all day, and I said, this is what you wanted.
> You wanted me to be a vegetable, not to have a mind of my own,
> how do you like it?
>   Billy was right. If I had been able to get a job, I would have
> been gone.

We have seen the many ways in which her partner effectively kept
Bernice out of the workplace through intimidation and violence, efforts
strangely identical to the approaches described by welfare-to-work service providers and domestic violence victims throughout the country,
and now beginning to be captured in formal research studies.

Sabotaging work isn't the only tool available to the abuser. Keeping his partner pregnant is another way to imprison her at home. But only recently has thinking about teen pregnancy been expanded to include the issue of domestic violence. Bernice's long struggle to use contraception and to maintain control over her own reproduction, to which we will now turn, illustrates the many ways that abusers use the issue of birth control as a means of domination.

CHAPTER THREE

Having Babies

> The fact, as I think we shall agree, is that women from the
> earliest times to the present day have brought forth the
> entire population of the universe. This occupation has taken
> much time and strength. It has also brought them into
> subjection to men.
>
> —VIRGINIA WOOLF, *"The Intellectual Status of Women"*

Bernice's two children were born in 1985 and 1989, when Bernice was twenty and twenty-three years of age. Although Bernice became pregnant as a teenager many times, she had a total of three miscarriages.

Bernice's doctor encouraged her to use birth control. Billy, however, was always against Bernice's using contraception. He used two basic approaches, of which the first was the argument that to use birth control is to become a slut: "The reason you want to use birth control is so you can be with other men." In the minds of many abusers, women who use birth control are able to have relationships with other men and not get "caught."

> *The issue of birth control brought about nasty fights. He would
> neglect me, he would stand off from me, he would say, "If you are
> going to take birth control, then maybe we shouldn't be together."*

In his many years of interviewing men accused of violent criminal acts, James Gilligan has described this particular attitude toward use of birth

control. Women, these men argue, dishonor their men by engaging in
sex outside the relationship:

> Men delegate to women the power to bring dishonor on
> men. . . . The most emotionally powerful means by which
> women can dishonor men is by engaging in nonmarital sex,
> i.e., by being too sexually active or aggressive. . . .
>
> We cannot think about preventing violence without a
> radical change in the gender roles to which men and women
> are subjected. The male gender role generates violence by
> exposing men to shame if they are not violent, and reward-
> ing them with honor if they are. The female gender role also
> stimulates male violence at the same time that it inhibits
> female violence. It does this by restricting women to the role
> of highly unfree sex objects, and honoring them to the de-
> gree that they submit to those roles or shaming them when
> they rebel. . . . It also encourages a man to become violent
> if the woman to whom he is related or married "dishonors"
> him by acting in ways that transgress her prescribed sexual
> role.[1]

Joan Haldeman, director of the Teen Mother Program at the Philadel-
phia Women's Association for Women's Alternatives, has informed me
that many of the girls in the program tell her they are afraid to address
birth control issues because they know that their partners will become
angry and they fear losing the relationship. That these men are not
really interested in children and do not want to be responsible for them
is proven by their subsequent demands that their partners undergo
abortions. "When she refused to have an abortion, one older guy said
he was going to stalk his partner until he could get her out where
nobody was around and beat the living daylights out of her because she
wouldn't have an abortion," explained Haldeman.[2]

Bernice also describes Billy's use of what she calls the "honey-
moon" approach: "Having a baby is going to bond us. We are going to
be together for the rest of our lives. The baby is a symbol of our love
for one another. If you loved me, you would have my child." Keeping
their women pregnant is an important method of control for batterers,
for women with many children or those who are constantly pregnant

48   will not be attractive to other men. More importantly, women who are constantly pregnant will be women out of the labor market.

So even though she didn't want a child, Bernice would stop using birth control. After the birth of her first child the same bitter arguments and physical abuse over birth control continued, with the result that Jessica was born three years later.

Just after Jessica's birth, Bernice had a tubal ligation and told Billy about it only afterward. When he found out about the surgery Billy left the hospital room and did not come back until it was time for Bernice to be discharged. As a result of the tubal ligation Billy felt betrayed and separated himself from his family for months at a time.

Research is beginning to support Bernice's experience with birth control and pregnancy. Among the first published studies was one undertaken by researchers from the Johns Hopkins University and the University of Florida, who held two focus groups in which women from domestic violence shelters were invited to take part in a discussion of partner violence and decisions about whether or not to become pregnant. According to most of the women, it was their partner who decided about birth control. One woman stated, "They own you when you have a child by him—part of the purpose in having a baby is to control you." Another woman stated that partners use "guns to control" or "they push you to have babies." "You can't always make decisions because all of your decision-making powers have been stripped away from you," said one participant. Another observed, "Once you have that first kid, then that makes you need them." Others described how their partners threw their birth control pills in the trash. Another told how she had to have three diaphragms so if her partner found one and threw it away, she would have another. The researchers concluded: "The results of this study clearly indicate connections between relationship abuse and unintended pregnancy through the partners' control of contraception and the man's pushing her to have a child. It is also clear that one means of abusive partners controlling their women is through having a child with them. The lack of using contraception also seemed to be related to the male partners' definition of manhood."[3]

Newly published research also confirms the universality of Bernice's experiences with birth control. Cycle Five of the National Survey of Family Growth obtained information from a national probability sample of 10,847 noninstitutionalized women ages fifteen to forty-four in 1995. The cycle included a measure of whether the girls' and women's first experience of sexual intercourse was voluntary and the degree to which the girls and women wanted it to occur. Importantly, Cycle Five collected data on the ages of the women's partners.

Although overall 91 percent of the girls and women reported that their first intercourse was voluntary, many nonetheless related the wantedness of the experience in the low or middle range; one-quarter gave low wantedness scores (one to four out of a scale of ten), indicating that although they had consented, they had not really wanted the intercourse to occur. Nine percent of women aged fifteen to twenty-four classified their first intercourse as nonvoluntary or rape. Nonvoluntary first intercourse occurred most frequently among those aged thirteen or younger. When the age of the partner was analyzed, the wantedness score decreased as the difference between the woman's age and that of her partner increased.

The study was able to examine associations between contraceptive use and varying degrees of wantedness of voluntary first intercourse. Women who had first intercourse with a man more than seven years older were less than half as likely to use contraceptives as women whose partners had been the same age or younger. In relationships with larger age discrepancies, the partners' advanced age worked against contraceptive use. "The fact that substantial numbers of young women voluntarily participated in a first sexual experience about which they felt ambivalent or negative deserves attention. It is especially salient for research and service programs, given that these 'voluntary but unwanted' experiences are most prevalent among young women whose youth or age difference with their partner decrease the likelihood of contraceptive use at first intercourse." This finding supports the notion that female power in a relationship correlates with contraceptive use; since domestic violence or abuse in these relationships indicates uneven power balances, it is likely that in relationships in which there is violence use of birth control would become an issue.[4]

In an effort to determine how to encourage condom use to protect against HIV and other sexually transmitted diseases, a recent study examined the consequences of having a physically abusive primary partner on condom use and sexual negotiation among young African American women. One hundred and sixty-five women ages eighteen to twenty-nine were recruited and interviewed between February and

50   December 1993 in a low-income neighborhood in San Francisco, California. Seventeen and a half percent of the sample reported having a physically abusive partner in the last three months.

The study found that women who were abused were more likely than others to report that their partner never used condoms (71 percent of the abused women versus about 43 percent of the nonabused). Abused women with a physically abusive partner stated that they were verbally abused, threatened with physical abuse, or threatened with abandonment when they asked their partner to use condoms at rates significantly higher than women whose partners were not abusive. Women with abusive partners were nine times more likely to be threatened with physical abuse when they asked their partner to use condoms as nonabused women, and battered women four times as likely to be threatened with abandonment.[5]

A yearlong study undertaken in collaboration with Planned Parenthood of Northern New Jersey involved open-ended interviews and focus groups with 127 male and female teens and adults. Girls in adult-teen relationships were found to be less likely to suggest or insist on contraception than were teens with teen partners, and they reported being intimidated by older partners regarding birth control issues. Importantly, girls stated that they were being pressured by adult partners to reverse decisions about terminating unwanted pregnancies, indicating the interest the male had in their partners' having children as a method of control. The researcher concluded: "In each of these cases, however, the adult male left during the pregnancy or shortly after the birth of a child. In many cases, girls reported cutting ties to school, families, or peers in order to please a jealous older partner, leaving themselves and their children particularly vulnerable when their partners left. Throughout the study, girls and women with experiences in adult-teen relationships noted problems due to power differences involving age, gender, and access to resources."[6]

Finally, a recent study of 150 black and Hispanic girls aged fourteen to seventeen found that, on average, girls whose first partners were at least three years older reported significantly younger ages of first intercourse than girls with peer-age first partners. Moreover, girls with older first partners were significantly less likely than girls with peer-age partners to have used birth control at first intercourse.[7]

Current theories explaining teen pregnancy fall into several distinct categories. Although there may be some truth to these approaches, no current theory integrates the issue of violence and the role abusers play in coercing pregnancies. Up to this moment, four basic approaches have dominated the debate about teen pregnancy.

1. *Lack of knowledge and access to family planning services is a major cause of teen pregnancy.* The theory goes like this: teenagers are not trying to become pregnant, but their lack of knowledge about reproduction and contraception, coupled with limited access to family planning services, means that they often engage in unprotected sexual activities. A large dent in this theory is starting to be made as the evidence continues to mount that early sexual intercourse is nonvoluntary for one in five girls, and that the younger a girl is when she first has sex, the more likely it is that her first sexual experience is not voluntary.[8]

2. *Early sexual intimacy and motherhood provide emotional closeness the girls are lacking.* One noted psychologist argues that if an adolescent's basic security needs have not been met, much of her time will be spent on resolving unmet dependency needs by searching for and trying to maintain attachments.

Girls for whom basic acceptance and love are the primary motivating forces have little interest or emotional energy to invest in school- or work-related activities unless they are exceptionally bright or talented. Even then, the pull of unmet affiliative or dependency needs may be more powerful than anything the worlds of school or work have to offer, particularly when these offerings are as inadequate and inconsistent as those typically found in poverty-stricken communities.

What must then be explained is how early parenthood meets similar developmental needs. Earlier sexual exploitation, along with the absence of appropriate male figures in fathering, "appear[s] to foster and fix a kind of learned helplessness in relationships with males." The victimized girl learns passivity and helplessness in relationship to men, because of the absence of appropriate male figures in fathering or grandfathering roles in her life:

> A failure to contracept can also be viewed as stemming in part from a sense that one's body is not really one's own. The capacity for self-care is largely derived from the internalization of experiences of being cared for and protected by caring others. Insistence that a partner contracept is pred-

icated on the ability to assert oneself and to stand up for one's rights. The diminished sense of personal worth and generalized hopelessness that characterizes many former victims would mitigate against such self-care and assertiveness.

Adolescent mothers frequently say that they had a child to hold onto a boyfriend or that they declined abortion or adoption at their boyfriend's urging. Still, the direction of male influence is anything but certain. We do not know if pressure from males is predominantly direct, indirect, or some combination of both. . . . Perhaps it would be better to conceptualize male influence as being less direct, serving more as an after-the-fact rationalization or as an added reason for keeping the child.[9]

Thus, the role played by men in wanting babies is acknowledged, but the author believes that the argument against male influence as a central force is the fact that girls break up with the fathers of the babies with great regularity. However, that the relationships do break up eventually is not a ground to believe that *at the time* the decision to have a child was not pushed on the women by their partners.

3. *Teen pregnancy is a rational response or a positive adaptation to adverse circumstances.* Because African Americans experience high rates of health problems in their late twenties and are more likely to receive aid from their families during their teen years, early childbearing is a rational choice:

> In fact, whether or not she marries before her first birth, a poor mother must expect to contribute substantially to the financial support of her children. But her chances for labor market attachment are also unreliable. If she finds employment, the wages and benefits she can command may not offset the costs of being a working mother. She cannot expect paid maternity leave; nor is accessible or affordable daycare available that would free her from reliance on kin for childcare once she does return to work. Moreover, she faces the social expectations that she help care for her kin as their health falters. Postponing childbearing increases the chance that her young children compete with ailing elders for her energies and decreases the chance that their father

will survive through much of their childhood. Her greatest
chance of long-term labor force attachment will be if her
children's pre-school years coincide with her years of peak
access to social and practical support provided by relatively
healthy kin. Her best chance of achieving her stated goals is
by becoming a mother at a young age.[10]

4. *As low-income teen parents fare no better or worse in the economy over time
than their nonpregnant counterparts, the fuss about teen pregnancy is overstated.* The
problem is not teen pregnancy but the conditions of poverty in which
these young women live: "A [poor] teenager who has a baby usually
adds but a slight burden to her life, which is already profoundly disadvantaged. . . . Early childbearing may make a bad situation worse, but
the real causes of poverty lie elsewhere." Americans want teenagers to
wait until they are mature to have sex and to delay until they are financially secure before they have children. Yet a great many girls will be
poor throughout their lives and will never be ready to be parents;
knowing this, the girls think, Why not have children now? "Society
should worry not about some epidemic of 'teenage pregnancy' but
about the hopeless, discouraged, and empty lives that early childbearing
denotes."[11]

To date, the failure to integrate what we now know about domestic
violence into the teen pregnancy debate is simply baffling. After review-
ing these theories, Rebekah Coley and Lindsay Chase-Lansdale usefully
note that economists, economic outcomes, and structural causes of poverty have dominated the discourse about teen pregnancy. They assert
that psychological theory is essential for understanding and responding
to the problem of teen pregnancy. Although teen pregnancy may not
alter the economic consequences for the girls, basic developmental
transformations that occur during adolescence, such as individuation
and identity formation and the ability to form mature, intimate relationships, are likely to be affected by early parenthood. "Virtually no
longitudinal and prospective studies have examined whether psychological factors such as self-esteem, individuation, or depression influence and are influenced by sexual activity and early childbearing, a
notable omission in the literature."[12]

As we have seen, Bernice's early life experiences led to teen pregnancy and a violent relationship that stunted her growth at the key

54 developmental time for her. As pointed out by Coley and Chase-Lansdale, we cannot prove that early sexual activity and childbearing influence issues of self-esteem, but we do know that they can lead to violent relationships, which do have such influence. It seems imperative for the teen pregnancy field to begin to integrate issues of violence into research and theory. To do so will dramatically change our fundamental view of low-income teen girls, from passive and helpless, without control of their own bodies, to girls like Bernice, who struggle, resist, and try to do what is morally correct and socially responsible, what they know to be right—which is not to bring into the world children they cannot support. Ultimately, however, many girls have to choose between use of birth control and the continuation of their intimate relationship, with often-predictable results.

All in all, Bernice says that there is no way one can overstate the importance of having babies for intimate partners who are abusers. Even to this day, years after the relationship has ended, Bernice's tubal ligation is on Billy's mind. Billy recently gloated to Bernice, "There is one great thing. Another man can't give you a baby." For an abuser, giving a woman a baby appears to be the ultimate act of control and possession.

Bernice now knows that her children's development was stunted by the violence in her home.

> Even as babies, they were the quietest children. My children never
> ran. Until a few years ago, I never saw them run, sweat, or play. I
> always knew there was something wrong with my kids. They shut
> down at a young age.

As a toddler Little Billy spent a lot of time huddled against the radiator in the apartment. At a year and a half, he got hold of a razor blade and cut his hands open. And he set fires. He would go outside and set paper on fire. He set his father's feet on fire. He set on fire the couch on which Bernice, nine months pregnant, was recumbent. And one time he set Jessica's bedroom on fire, with Jessica trapped in the room. Once Bernice left Billy, the fire-setting ceased.

Little Billy's therapist later told Bernice that her son very much wanted to stop the violence in his home, but as a child he could not prevent his father from abusing his mother. This sense of powerlessness greatly affected Little Billy's view of the world and his place in it. He became a child with little sense of personal efficacy and a great deal of anger. Little Billy was trying to bring the ugliness to a halt by burning the house down.

Because of his daydreaming, Little Billy's schoolwork was erratic. For a time he was in special education classes. Little Billy's handwriting was unlike that of most children's. For a long time he made his letters so small they could barely be read. Bernice says it was like he was trying to fit his thoughts inside a tiny box.

Jessica simply did not talk, saying hardly anything until she was almost four years old. Today Bernice remarks that she never realized, because of her isolation from others, that Jessica wasn't developing her speech as she should. Billy never let anyone else take care of the children. The only person around Jessica much was Bernice's mother, whose alcoholic state prevented her from noticing something like that.

Both children also had serious asthma attacks. Little Billy had his first severe asthma episode at eleven months. Every three to four months he needed hospitalization for at least six days to recover from his latest severe attack. Only after Bernice finally found a way to leave Billy did her children's asthma attacks trail off.

Given the odds against her, then how did Bernice manage her escape, and what can we learn from it in order to help others like her?

CHAPTER FOUR

Leaving

> You have won rooms of your own in the house hitherto
> exclusively owned by men. You are able, though not
> without great labour and effort, to pay the rent. You are
> earning your five hundred pounds a year. But this freedom
> is only a beginning; the room is your own, but it is still
> bare. It has to be furnished; it has to be decorated; it has to
> be shared. How are you going to furnish it, how are you
> going to decorate it? With whom are you going to share it,
> and upon what terms?
>
> —VIRGINIA WOOLF, *"Professions for Women"*

Bernice finally left Billy for good in early January 1993. Like a lot of other survivors of domestic violence, Bernice left only because the fear no longer became a factor. Put another way, the fear reached a new dimension. Death seemed preferable to living with such fear and violence. This insight freed Bernice to risk her own life in order to build a new world for herself and the children.

Another rape was the precipitating crisis. Although there was so much rape throughout the relationship, Bernice says that particular rape was unbearable.

> *That night when he raped me, I had so many pictures going through
> my mind. . . . I just felt so filthy, I felt so invaded, it is the most
> awful feeling in the world to not even have your own body, and I*

couldn't take it any more. I actually imagined myself hurting him,
I wanted to stab him, I wanted to choke him. There was such a rage
that came over me that I dreamed of him being dead all night.

I actually came outside myself and was afraid that I couldn't
get back to myself. It was so clear, like I was actually sitting there
talking with two different individuals, and I said if I can pull myself
back together I promise I will leave this whole situation. I will never
come back. I want my body. If I can't have anything else, I am
going to have my body. I just could not live like that another day. A
lot of strength came from that.

The next morning Bernice found herself in a trance. When in that state
she doesn't know what has happened and cannot remember what has
occurred. Later Bernice's therapist explained to her that these trances
were her body's way of protecting herself; during the trances the mind
gets reintegrated after a violent episode. While in the trance, however,
Bernice was always afraid that she was never going to come out of it.
Bernice thinks she started going into trances as a child whenever her
mother started to drink. Then Bernice would just fade out so she
wouldn't have to remember her mother drinking herself insensible.
Now Bernice realizes that if she is afraid of something she can call up a
trance if she feels traumatized. "I can safely deal with it. I know that I
can come back. I know I am not going to get lost."

"Divine intervention" came the next day with two visits. In the
morning came Monique, a friend Bernice had made in nursing training.
Monique said, "What's wrong with you? I've never seen you like this,"
and burst into tears. Bernice snapped out of her trance and told Monique of the previous night's rape. Monique kept repeating, "Bernice,
what is holding you here? What is holding you here?"

Next came Bernice's case manager, Denise Innis. Bernice says that
by this time she was seriously suicidal.

I was afraid to open that door. I thought it was a trick that Billy
was going to see if I would answer the door when he wasn't there. It
was Denise. It went straight through me. I had so many emotions
rushing at me. Denise said to me a couple of times, "Get dressed.
You need to leave this house." I was so afraid, and when I came out
of the house I was so paranoid. We went driving, we just went

driving. I rolled down the window and I felt like something had
grabbed hold of me. Denise was talking to me but I couldn't hear
anything she was saying. I felt so free, and when I went back to the
house I felt like I had become a person again.

Because Bernice did not feel it was safe for her family to be involved in
her escape, it was Denise who had found her a bed in a battered wom-
en's shelter. But Denise's plan to get to the shelter, which involved
summoning the police to her home, seemed unworkable to Bernice,
who didn't think the police would protect her and didn't want the
children witnessing another potentially violent confrontation. Bernice
decided instead to go home and get herself out.

When she returned home, Billy and his brother were there, getting
high. Billy invited Bernice to join in. While they were smoking the
marijuana Bernice wasn't inhaling it, but just blowing the smoke out
and praying that it wouldn't affect her mind.

I told him today is mothers' and daughters' day and I had to take
the baby to the welfare-to-work program with me. I knew he was
going to be suspicious. Little Billy was in school. So I went to him
and said, "I'm going on to school, but don't forget to pick me up so
I don't have to walk all the way back with the baby." And so,
because he was already high and he didn't want to take me to school,
he says, "Just go, but I am not going to take you." And if I didn't
make a point of asking him to come to pick me up, it would seem
suspicious.

So I got the bag and took the baby and went to Little Billy's
school, and I got him and his school records. I spoke with the principal, and he was really wonderful about helping. I got on the Chicago
Avenue bus, took it to Pulaski, took the Pulaski bus to North Avenue,
and then the North Avenue bus to the shelter. They knew who I was
when I got there, and when I arrived I threw the bag on the floor
and began to cry. The entire trip took forty-five minutes but to me
it felt like a six- to seven-hour journey. They couldn't even do intake
on me. They saw how exhausted I was. They took my children and
put them in with the rest of the children, showed me where they
were, and took me to my room. I fell asleep immediately.

Bernice explains that during her escape it seemed that she was sleep-walking, in a daze, numbed, and going through the motions.

> It is amazing how the mind can protect you. If I had been in touch
> with my reality, I would have been too paralyzed with fear. Instead,
> I was almost euphoric, like I was high on drugs. Time was so
> different for me. It seemed like it had been hours, an all-day thing.
> When I came out of that state, I was scared to death. It didn't seem
> real. It didn't seem like it had been done. Mentally it was somebody
> else who did it.

As a result, Bernice had trouble adjusting.

> When I woke up I was all in a sweat. I was trying to get out, I
> thought I was at home, I thought he had caught me. I was petrified.
> When I came to my senses, it was such a shock, and I walked around
> in shock for a whole week. The only thing that helped me was the
> noonday visit from Denise. She got permission to come into the
> shelter. That allowed me to know that I did have an outside world.
> It just didn't seem real to me. Billy always told me that wherever
> you go, I will find you, and that is what I always believed. I knew
> that leaving him meant dying. But it was okay. I was ready to die.
> I couldn't live that way anymore. If that was what it was going to
> take, it was okay.

Bernice left with the clothes on her back and thirteen dollars in her pocket. She also remembers how cold it was that January day, with rain later changing to freezing rain and snow. "That is why he was so shocked that I left. A woman to leave with two children and thirteen dollars in the middle of winter. She can't go anywhere, he thinks. She's stuck."

When Bernice left the shelter, she returned to her mother's apartment until a subsidized flat became available in another neighborhood. That first year Bernice had no furniture and the family slept on the floor. They had a table, a TV, a stove, and a refrigerator. It didn't matter because she had her peace. Bernice was saving money for a car.

> I lived in that apartment for a whole year, and I had a problem with
> my shower and I had to call the landlord to send someone over. A

Mr. *Winfield came and fixed the shower. He looked around kindly,
and said, "Ms. Hampton, I just wanted to ask you, when do you
intend to buy some furniture?" I said, "What do you mean?" "You
don't have curtains on your windows, you have the newspaper there.
You could make your apartment a whole lot softer and homier. That
would be very good for you and your children." Do you believe this?
I had not even realized it.*

Bernice's sister, Brenda, today marvels at Bernice's determination then:

You could have gone to Daddy's house, or Momma's house,
or my house, but you wanted to protect the family. You said,
"This is my battle, I've got to come through by myself." You
were so determined. That fear was so strong that it kind of
helped you in a way, because you didn't want to live that
way anymore. It carried you a long way, that fear did, because eventually it became a positive force in your life because it drove you to fight this man. You stood up to your
biggest fear, and you overcame it, that is what you did.

Even today, years later, Bernice can remember that intoxicating sense
of freedom she experienced while in shelter. One night she and another
woman decided to walk to a store to buy some needed items for the
children. On the way back it started to pour, and she and her friend
had to run through the rain to return to the shelter. Bernice was sur-
prised that there were no adverse consequences; the only thing that
happened was that she dried herself off. Nobody yelled at her or punished her for being dumb enough to walk in the rain.

*There was nobody asking me where I was going, what did I do. It
just freaked me out. I went into the room and I just sat there on the
bed, totally amazed that I had done this. That I had some freedom
to make my own choices. I then made a decision. I wanted to be
free. I didn't want to be controlled. Thirteen years was long enough.
Now I want my own life. I can still feel that rain on my face
even now.*

Unfortunately, it is often more dangerous for battered women after they leave a violent relationship. Although divorced and separated women compose only 10 percent of all women in this country, they account for three-quarters of all battered women. Divorced and separated women report being physically abused fourteen times as often as women still living with their partners.[1] In a recent national survey in Canada, approximately one in five women (19 percent) who reported violence by an intimate partner claimed that the violence occurred during or after separation. In just over one in three cases (35 percent) the severity of violence had increased at the time of separation.[2]

The first comprehensive report on the prevalence of stalking in the United States, published in 1997, involved a probability sample of eight thousand women and eight thousand men who were surveyed about their experiences of stalking. It found that one out of every twelve women in America, or 8.2 million women, have been stalked sometime in their lifetime. Most of the stalking occurred after the intimate relationship had terminated. Twenty-one percent of these victims said the stalking happened before the relationship ended, 43 percent reported that it occurred after the relationship terminated, and 36 percent said it happened before and after the relationship ended. Stalkers were also abusers. Eighty-one percent of the women who were stalked by husbands or cohabiting partners were physically assaulted by the same partners, and 31 percent of the women who were stalked by husbands or cohabiting partners were sexually assaulted by the same partner. Husbands or partners who stalked their partners were four times more likely than husbands or partners in the general population to physically assault their partners and were six times more likely than husbands and partners in the general population to sexually assault their partners.

Over a quarter (26 percent) of the stalking victims said their victimization caused them to lose time from work. Seven percent stated that they never returned to work. About a third of the women and a fifth of the men stated they sought psychological counseling as a result of their stalking victimization. Nor was the stalking of short duration. On average, stalking cases last 1.8 years, with about two-thirds continuing a year or less, and approximately a quarter persisting two to five years. About a tenth of all stalking cases last more than five years. In addition, stalking cases involving intimates or former intimates lasted, on average, twice as long as stalking cases involving nonintimates.[3]

Homicide data reveal high percentages of battered women as victims, and many of the victims had left their abuser at the time of their
death. In a recent study of homicide victims in New York City by the
City Department of Health, intimate partner and family homicides con-
stituted 49 percent of all homicides of women between 1900 and 1994
in which the motive was known. Fifty-two percent of the women were
not living with their boyfriends or their husbands at the time of the
homicide.[4] In an analysis of Canadian homicide data between 1974 and
1992, married women were nine times more likely to be killed by their
spouse than by a stranger. Separation presented a sixfold increase in risk
to women in comparison to couples who continued to reside together.[5]

Male threats of suicide during stalking episodes also play a large
role, and they make domestic violence victims feel guilty. The Worcester Family Research Project found that about 46 percent of the abusers
in its sample threatened to kill themselves.[6] As Bernice explains: "Once
he realizes that she is gone and isn't going to come back, the abuser is
willing to commit suicide and even murder because he is afraid to go
on with his life."

All too often the threat is real. In 1996 I interviewed a social worker
in the Kearns, Utah, welfare department office who told me of one of
his recent cases. He had been counseling a mother of two (with a third
child on the way) whose abusive partner would not let her get a job.
When she told him she was leaving, her partner pointed a gun at her
womb and then shot and killed himself in front of her and the two
children. The woman suffered a miscarriage induced by the shock.[7]

As I am writing this, a newspaper reports that a financial adviser,
Donna Powell, escaped death by a fraction of an inch when David Furby
shot her through the neck after she said she was leaving him. He then
killed himself. Powell stated that Furby couldn't bear the thought of
losing her because he loved her so much. "I was his life. I have to live
with the knowledge that if I hadn't told him I wanted to separate he
would never have done this. I made him do it; I feel terribly guilty."
Recording a verdict of suicide, the coroner said that Mr. Furby "seems
to have been unhinged by his jealousy to the point of losing his mind."[8]

Consider also the case of Betty Clark. In September 1995 she, her
three children, and her ex-husband, Mark Clark, were killed as a result
of Mark's installing and detonating bombs in his car. Betty had agreed
to meet Mark one last time to take the children for school clothes.

Betty was near the end of a process that, she hoped, would make her independent and capable of supporting her family on her own. After leaving her husband, Betty earned her GED from a local welfare-to-work program and subsequently moved to the Baltimore, Maryland, area, where she was studying to become a medical secretary at the time of her death. One acquaintance told the *Baltimore Sun*, "If he couldn't have her and watch those kids grow up, no one else could."[9]

A recent case from South Florida also illustrates how stalking disrupts employment for domestic violence survivors. Amy Hall, a forty-four-year-old mother of one, worked as a teacher's assistant at an average weekly wage of $368. Her duties included summer camp counseling and after-school child care. Within weeks after she married, Hall became the victim of domestic abuse and rape. Her husband began his stalking after Hall made a trip to the courthouse to obtain a restraining order. He came to her school, putting the children at risk. He made incessant calls to her beeper or answering machine. The state's attorney's office advised Hall to quit her job and her apartment for good and go into hiding. Although she did do just that, Ms. Hall struggled with bouts of depression and other lingering psychological effects of the ordeal and had difficulty making ends meet.[10]

Bernice's longtime partner also became her stalker, with serious repercussions for her welfare-to-work journey. When Bernice left the shelter and moved back to her mother's house, Billy found her, and the stalking began. Billy stalked Bernice everywhere she went. Often he spent the night outside her apartment, silently watching.

Just after she left the shelter, I offered Bernice a job we had available at the Chicago Commons Employment Training Center as a part-time case manager, where she was to work with other victims of domestic violence. About six months later, I helped Bernice obtain a second part-time job with a nearby community organization.

During this time, however, Billy's stalking intensified. Even though Bernice did not hesitate to call the police when it occurred, the criminal justice system didn't seem to deter Billy. "After he was arrested," says Bernice, "he would come out of the police station and say, 'You don't get the message. There is nothing that anyone can do to me. I will always get out. And when I get out, what do you think you are going to get?' " Then he would choke Bernice on the street across from the police station.

> The stalking came out of jealousy. He did not want me to succeed.
> He did not want me to have anything. Everything I had he wanted
> to take away from me. I was going to the grocery store and I had
> two bags of groceries. He stalked me, and he would knock my grocer-
> ies out of my hand and go about his business. He was being vindic-
> tive. "How much can I hurt you? How can I get at you? How can
> I stop you from sleeping at night?"

Most days Billy stalked Bernice as she was waiting for the bus to go to work. Many were the times he dragged Bernice into the mud. Routinely she would get up, go to work, and head for the bathroom to clean herself off. One time as Bernice was being pursued by Billy near the bus stop, she ran into a convenience store. The woman at the cash register told Bernice to lock herself in the bathroom and she would call the police. Before the police officers came, Billy had knocked a great many groceries from the shelves. After the police came and arrested her former partner, Bernice took the bus to work, never telling anyone about the incident.

Bernice now says that the time of the stalking was the worst period of her entire life. The stalking, she explains, was different from the domestic violence. When she lived with Billy, Bernice could control the violence by complying with what he wanted. But the stalking wasn't about control. Billy didn't want Bernice back. "His state of mind was totally different. It was about punishment. 'I'm depressed. I don't have any reason to live. Why should you live?' "

Bernice felt she couldn't control Billy's actions. It wasn't about giv-ing him anything, it was about his wanting to take. She had no control over what Billy would do to vindicate himself. For a year and a half, Bernice says, she lived in absolute terror.

Even when he assaulted her when they were still together, Billy didn't hit Bernice with all his strength. When he stalked her, his blows were harder. Bernice seriously believed that her life was in danger.

> He was truly meaning to hurt and torture me, and that explains the
> sitting in the park outside, the knocking on the doors, sitting on the

back porch, hammering on the door late at night, coming to the job,
waiting for me at the bus stops. When he came into that Seven-
Eleven store, he was a madman.

Moreover, Bernice explains that she had so many responsibilities as a
single mother and on the job that she couldn't really disassociate herself
for long periods of time before she was called upon to do something.
So she had to live with the terror. Bernice did not answer the telephone
or open the door if the bell rang.

> All of us slept in one room. We slept in that one room because I was
> afraid to let those kids that far from me, and I chose the back room,
> which is a small child's room, because it was closer to the door. As
> big as that apartment is, it was like there was really only one room
> in that house. He had forced us into one room.

To make matters worse, Bernice did not want any of us at work to learn
about the stalking. Now, many years later, I ask Bernice why she kept
the stalking hidden from us. She says she didn't want other people to be
afraid to be around her. Bernice didn't and doesn't want to be labeled as
a victim at work.

> I want them to see me as a person who is capable, who has good
> ideas. If they view me as a victim, they don't have to address the
> concerns I have at work because they feel my emotions are out of
> place. People try to manipulate me through that. People underesti-
> mate me. They say, "Oh, Bernice, just calm down." They then draw
> back from me. So I am hiding it once again. I have to. I don't want
> to be a professional victim.

When we were talking about the stalking, I suddenly remembered that
on many evenings I would drive Bernice from the office part of the way
home—not all of the way, because the route did take me out of my
way. But when I dropped her at the bus stop at Central and Augusta, I
thought I had considerably shortened her journey. What I didn't know
was that I had made Bernice's return home much more secure. Now I
feel bad that most of the time I did not go out of my way slightly to
deliver her to her door. Why didn't she tell me? "No, no," Bernice

66   says. "It was the image. I wanted to fit in. I wanted to be a worker. I
never wanted you to know."

Even now, Bernice remains angry that it is not possible for her to
reveal her problems at the workplace.

> I work in a social service environment, yet I'm not allowed to have
> problems or be a real human being. It is just so contradictory to me.
> I don't have a lot of pride. I don't mind allowing people to see my
> problems, but I don't want to be judged or be put down. Where I
> work, people just don't want to know. They're having their own
> problems, and you're having yours, and we stay divided.

Billy blew her game the day he choked Bernice in front of our office.
At the time, Bernice explained that Billy wasn't really trying to kill her.
He wanted us to see the attack so Bernice would lose her job. "He was
so angry. He wanted revenge. That is what stalking is all about. Whenever I opened a door in my life, he wanted to close it."

As part of the punishment Billy inflicted on Bernice he would not
return the children after visitation, which the judge had authorized after
she ordered Billy to provide child support. One time Bernice tracked
the children down at Billy's aunt's house and had to threaten to call the
police to have the children released to her.

Bernice realized that although she had moved on, Billy was still
stuck in the violence cycle. Her court order required Billy to provide
medical benefits for the children. When he did not take care of this,
Bernice spoke with Billy about the matter.

> He said, "When you walked and took them away from me, you
> took everything. You don't deserve anything." I am asking for some-
> thing for the children, and he says that I do not deserve it. These are
> his children, but he is viewing the whole thing as domestic violence,
> as punishing me. I realized that he is still living in that world. He
> has not woken up.

For Bernice, the most frightening thing was leaving work at the end of
the day. Obtaining a driver's license and an automobile was an important element in Bernice's securing her own safety and that of the children. I will never forget the day that Bernice passed her driving test.

She tore into our office and waltzed around with the license held over her head like a trophy. The smile went from ear to ear. That driver's license symbolized Bernice's freedom. Only when she purchased her first automobile—a used clunker—did she feel truly safe going from home to work.

During the stalking both children's asthma attacks became more serious. The first time that Billy came to the apartment and tried to break in, Jessica developed breathing problems. The next day Bernice took her daughter to the county hospital, where the child, in serious condition, landed in intensive care for a week. That same day Little Billy also had a severe asthma attack; unfortunately for Bernice, he had to be admitted to a different hospital, the one at which his doctor practiced.

Bernice kept to her schedule of working her two part-time jobs. No one at either job knew her two children were hospitalized. After work Bernice ran from one hospital to the other. Little Billy was the first to be released. Bernice brought her son with her to Jessica's hospital because the stalking made her fear to leave Little Billy with anyone. But because she was not allowed to bring him into the intensive care unit, Bernice had to leave Little Billy unattended in the waiting area. Meanwhile, Billy had followed Bernice to the hospital, which increased her terror. She was afraid that he would interfere with Jessica or grab Little Billy from the waiting room. To make matters worse, Bernice was petrified that Billy, blaming her for the children's medical condition, would seek to obtain custody of the children.

"I lost fifteen pounds in that two-week period," explains Bernice. "I didn't get home until nine-thirty at night and I simply didn't eat at all." Adding to the stress was the refusal of the state's medical assistance program to pay for Little Billy's new medication, which cost $237 per week. Bernice finally arranged for the medication to be paid through a private foundation.

The children never had serious asthma attacks once Billy stopped stalking Bernice. And when the stalking stopped, the children really started to grow. For years, Little Billy and Jessica had grown slowly, and the children wore the same clothes for two years at a time. Bernice says they never had much of an appetite, but they are making up for it now. "Wouldn't you know it, they really started to eat as soon as I became ineligible for food stamps," Bernice ruefully exclaims. Once the stalking stopped, Bernice found, like other mothers, that she had to purchase new clothes at the start of the summer and winter seasons.

The children's school was extremely supportive of Bernice and Little Billy during the time she was being stalked.

> They had such sympathy. I am being stalked, but my child had
> perfect attendance. They were very welcoming. All the mothers had
> to wait outside for the children, but I could come right in, wait in
> the office, or go upstairs and wait in the classroom. Anytime they
> saw me, school security would come to assist.

Bernice says that the teachers worked hard to bring out Little Billy. The school authorities saw a child with perfect attendance and perfect dress and hygiene, but they also observed a quiet and depressed child. Gradually the school tried to get Little Billy to participate in activities. He was appointed a hall monitor, and the more responsibility he had, the more he blossomed. Bernice remembers the time that Little Billy was selected to give a speech over the school intercom to the students during African American Heritage month. Bernice came to the school to hear him proudly deliver the speech he had written himself.

At the time of the stalking Jessica was in an all-day child care program. Jessica's teacher noticed that the little girl wasn't talking or interacting with the other children. When her motor and language skills were tested, Jessica was found to be developmentally delayed. Bernice shared her background with the child care center, and a speech therapist began to work with Jessica at the site. The experts believed that Jessica's speech was being delayed and sabotaged by the violence and the stalking. Jessica had become another silent woman, already in danger of becoming dependent and subject to abuse in later life.

Although Jessica made progress, today Bernice thinks more strides would have been possible at that time if she herself hadn't been stalked.

> I was just going through the motions. I was too terrified to be able
> to interact with and converse with my children. Our house was quiet
> all the time. The only time the kids would really talk was if you put
> us in one room and closed the door. My only interaction with people
> was at my job. Besides that, I spent all my evenings and weekends
> alone.

At home Bernice found that the children were beginning to run out of control. Little Billy and Jessica weren't minding her, the two children were continually fighting with one another, and Little Billy wasn't coming home on time and was stealing from stores. Since Bernice didn't believe in physical punishment, she was at a loss in dealing with them. To make matters worse, Little Billy obviously feared that Bernice would become involved in another abusive situation. For this reason he didn't want Bernice ever leaving the house or interacting with outside people. "We were all supposed to live in this little bubble together," she explains. So Little Billy became Bernice's new abuser and controller.

Bernice obtained counseling for the children. There she learned that they too were violence victims who needed to participate in a recovery process. Today, Little Billy's therapist says that the boy had to learn to express his feelings. On the inside he had been very angry about the violence that had gone on in the household and his inability to stop his father from abusing his mother. The therapist worked with Little Billy to learn to express his feelings and not let the anger build up. Building verbal skills is necessary, continues the therapist, if Little Billy is going to "learn these techniques to reduce violence and anger that have been a part of him, so that he will not be a perpetrator himself in the future."

Jessica also had the same problem, although typically for a girl, she expressed it differently. Jessica, her therapist says, really couldn't talk about anything. "Jessica did not open up and talk. Anything I asked, she would simply reply 'Everything is fine.' We knew it wasn't fine. But at first she wouldn't talk about anything." Jessica was in deep academic trouble. Because of her nightmares and her daydreaming, she simply wasn't able to take in any new information. Even at this early age, Jessica had simply shut down.

Studies have shown that despite mothers' efforts to shield their children from violence, 68 to 87 percent of the incidents of domestic violence are, in fact, witnessed by children. Research now demonstrates that children exposed to the battering of their mothers suffer the same harm and display the same symptoms as children who are actually abused, including the symptoms of posttraumatic stress disorder. Such trauma damages children's capacity to trust, leaves them hypervigilant, impairs their ability to manage tension, frustration, and transition, and adversely affects their schoolwork and social relationships. Preschoolers exposed to domestic violence exhibit trauma symptoms that include

70   insomnia, sleepwalking, nightmares and bed-wetting, headaches, stomachaches, diarrhea, ulcers, and asthma.[11]

School-age children often have difficulties in school, including poor academic performance, school phobia, and troubles with concentration. They have an increased tendency to fight with peers, rebel against instruction and authority, or exhibit an unwillingness to complete schoolwork. Many suffer low self-esteem, sadness, depression, poor impulse control, and feelings of powerlessness. In a study in 1985, the Boston Department of Youth Services found that children of abused mothers were six times more likely to attempt suicide, 74 percent more likely to commit crimes against the person, twenty-four times more likely to have committed sexual assault crimes, and 50 percent more likely to abuse drugs or alcohol than children whose mothers were not battered.[12]

⚜

Patti Davis, executive director of a battered women's service program in Wichita, Kansas, recently described to me how her ex-husband's stalking, like Bernice's, affected her efforts to become self-sufficient. Patti's partner didn't let her use the telephone, drive the car, receive a letter, or go to church. The two times during her ten-year union that she tried to go to work he sabotaged her efforts, even though he himself was mostly unemployed, or at best seasonally employed, and had difficulty in supporting his family.

Eventually Patti grabbed an opportunity and fled the state of Colorado, returning with her children to her parents' home in Kansas. Her husband soon followed, at which point he tried to kill her, injured her father, and was arrested numerous times. Patti says that for the first year the fear was simply overwhelming: "He threatened to kill me, and I thought he would be successful. The kids went to school, my parents went to work, and I sat in the house in the dark in my bathrobe all day long, depressed and in shock."

During this first year Patti applied for welfare to help support herself and her children. A year later she went back to college at Wichita State University and later began a job with the county. Throughout, Patti's ex-husband stalked and threatened to kill her, fought for custody of the children, and even kidnapped one of the kids and took him to Colorado. Like Bernice, Patti had to cope with all this, including numerous legal actions, at the same time she was holding down her very first job.

Unlike Bernice, Patti decided she had better inform everyone at work about her situation. She says that if she had kept the domestic violence a secret, that would be yet another thing her ex-husband could hold over her head. And because he came to the job to harass her, everyone knew about it anyway. Yet Patti believes her truthfulness about her situation was bad for her professionally: "I could never convince myself that my co-workers didn't think of me as someone who couldn't handle the job and the responsibility. I got defined by being a victim. Although I had responsibility, I never got promoted or a salary increase over the years. I think it hurt me to be so open about it on the job. Yet I thought it was important not to be ashamed of my situation."

And like Bernice, Patti tells me that she thinks that the time after leaving the violent relationship was the most frightening. "It was a really scary time," she says today. Patti believes that too many services are focused on helping women leave violent relationships and not enough community-based support is available to women like herself and Bernice after they leave and attempt to work. When women are depressed and frightened as they are being stalked, she says, it is difficult for them to stay strong and committed to "staying gone," as Bernice expresses it. [13]

Billy stopped stalking Bernice after a year and a half. Why then did the stalking finally stop? Bernice says that Billy kept following her, grabbing her on the street, and pulling her into alleys and beating her. Although she consistently called the police, it was having no effect. Finally one day Bernice reached the point of no return.

> I thought he was going to kill me. I had gotten to that point in my mind that it was okay. If I die tomorrow, I did everything that I could. I wasn't afraid to die. I didn't want to die, but I wasn't afraid. So, as Billy attacked me once again, I told him, "Go ahead and kill me. I am not going to back off." It finally made an impact on him. Once he heard that I was not afraid to die, he realized he didn't have the same control over me. I wasn't going to quit.

Billy's power over Bernice—her fear—had been broken. And luckily, Billy, as it would later become clear, did not really want to go so far as to kill Bernice or himself.

CHAPTER FIVE

Recovering: Is There a "Culture of Poverty"?

I mark Henry James's sentence: Observe perpetually.
Observe the oncome of age. Observe greed. Observe my
own despondency. By that means it becomes serviceable. Or
so I hope.

—VIRGINIA WOOLF, *The Diary of Virginia Woolf*

What does it take for victims of domestic violence to recover from its effects? Bernice's struggles with recovery while she was working can do much to inform policy and services for battered women on welfare.

According to Richard Davenport-Hines, the poet W. H. Auden hated twentieth-century self-pity: "He was suspicious of creeds of personal development and distrusted the introspective tendencies in himself and other people. Auden thought their result was too often to make people sorry for themselves and diminish their powers of free choice. Neuroses, he decided in 1919, should be welcomed as a potential source of strength and originality; they should vitalise people rather than weaken them."[1]

For full recovery from violence to occur, Auden's approach is on the mark: victims must transmute the negative effects of their victimhood into strengths, a process requiring rebuilding of self-esteem, integration of the experience into the psyche, and a moving on. I can always tell whether a woman is in the recovery process if she is able to speak of her own strengths instead of dwelling on the trauma of the past. Annie Boone, a survivor of domestic violence from Salt Lake City, Utah: "I have to depend on me. I am my own best friend." Another survivor: "Now I can realize my personal power. I understand how I got into this situation."[2]

For the first few years, Bernice says, it was difficult for her to put the past out of her mind, indicating that she had not completed the task of finding a way to go on with her life.

> I still cried at night. I still had nightmares. I still dreamed that I was with him, and my dreams were more real to me than the life that I was actually living. It was really hard to go on. I was living like I was going to wake up and everything was going to be gone and I would be still with him. I hadn't accepted that this was my life, that I had made these changes, because when you have lived a certain way for ten years, and then almost two years later there is a really big change, you will not accept those two years as opposed to those ten years. I was still living in those ten years. My growth was slow because of my own denial. Life didn't seem real to me. Every day that I go through my life it seems like one day I'm going to wake up and it is all going to be gone.

According to trauma experts, women like Bernice are exchanging one identity with another. "If women tend to define themselves in the context of relationships, then it is not surprising that women making a break with their pasts and former relationships may enter a period in which there is considerable flux in self-concept. . . . They feel trapped by the negative images from the past or splintered into vaguely sensed parts and subject to kaleidoscopic shifts in self-picture that kept them off balance."[3] In short, violence victims such as Bernice are subject to a "cognitive cloudiness." They are unsure if they really know what they seem to know and if their achievements are genuinely deserved. They have to develop a sense of subjective self, an idea of their own inner power, and a realization that they have the strength to reason, make decisions, and listen to their own intuition and inner voice.

Flashbacks and disassociation, which interfere with daily life, can also be continuous problems for victims. In interviews compiled in

74   Utah, Pat, a former violence victim, describes how memories currently interfere with her daily functioning:

> The last Valentine's Day we were together and my husband had raped me. This Valentine's Day the memory came up and hit me over the head. I was almost catatonic—it was just leftover trauma. It's really difficult to put your life together again because there's so much pressure to survive, to provide food and clothing for your child. If you try to do that and don't deal with the psychological issues at the same time, it's self-defeating. Someday that stuff will catch up with you. Leaving—it's not just walking out one day and okay, that's the end of it.
>
> I've been out three years in March, and I'm just starting to deal with the trauma. It's difficult for me to trust anybody. I assume if anybody promises to do something, they'll probably back out of it. Even normal interaction with people is exhausting. There's no way you can rebuild your life in two years.[4]

Bernice believes that her habit of disassociation affected her cognitive abilities. "Domestic violence slows you down. It is as if you don't have any ability to learn. Your mind shuts down. You learn at a slower rate. Your mind doesn't want anything because it knows that it can't have it. It is better just to shut down." In the past it could take Bernice as long as three months to read a book that she can now complete in less than a week. Recently I was excited to hear that Bernice had read a fairly hefty paperback book in just one weekend.

If we fail to take into account the complexity and difficulty of the recovery process, we can cause untold harm for women and children who are survivors of domestic violence. Some women who choose or are forced to work while the recovery process is underway may fail, and professional support and assurance could substantially help many.

During her first few months at work Bernice had a difficult time. She explains that she had no confidence that she could do the work. Today Bernice recalls the terror of her first few weeks on the job, which she needed badly. She was given assignments but had no idea how to perform them. She also had no way of knowing what would be reasonable expectations for an employee like herself. What was she supposed to know, and when was it reasonable for her to ask for clarification? Since Bernice was afraid she would be fired if she revealed her inadequacy, she simply did not ask anything. One of her first tasks was to telephone program participants who hadn't come recently and hadn't had communication with the school.

> I didn't know how to talk to the clients. I didn't know what to say
> to them. I was so confused and scared, and I didn't know where to
> begin. When I would call someone's home and there would be any
> problem, I would just hang up. I didn't know how to communicate
> with people. What forced me to do it is that I said to myself, "If I
> don't do it, then I'll be fired, so start talking." I didn't want to ask
> my supervisor how to do it. I thought that maybe it was something
> that was common knowledge to talk on the phone. I didn't want her
> to think that she hired someone who couldn't do basic things.

One of Bernice's other early tasks was to telephone different organizations to locate social service resources for the program's participants.

> I would call and say I was looking for a domestic violence shelter.
> The person would say, "Who are you?" She thought I was a client.
> I didn't know I was supposed to introduce myself and the purpose of
> my call. I learned that from the people I called. When a person
> would come on the line and give her name, identifying herself as the
> shelter's intake worker, I said to myself, oh, titles! It was a whole
> training process in every area of my job to figure out how to do the
> task on my own. And it was hard to remain focused because of the
> stalking. But I learned to train myself. Once I was in the building,
> I realized that I was safe. After a while I never wanted the end of the
> workday to come, because I would get to the bus stop and there he
> would be.

Still, Bernice remained mortally afraid of looking dumb. She says that most of her learning occurred through eavesdropping. She listened to her supervisor's telephone conversations and sessions with program participants. Bernice says she learned how to talk by watching others and copying their behavior. Eventually, her supervisor showed Bernice

76   how to take notes so she could refer to them and didn't have to keep everything in her head.

As a result of her past trauma, Bernice's responses to different situations at the workplace were plainly inappropriate. If her supervisor was criticizing her, Bernice found herself withdrawing or disassociating from the situation as she had done in the past when Billy was coming at her. Any criticism, however constructive, paralyzed her. "I wouldn't talk, but I would cry and cry, and my crying would be uncontrollable. She would try to say to me, 'This is not personal, Bernice. You need to develop skills.' "

Now Bernice says she knows that she was overreacting, but her own mind's defense mechanisms came automatically into play. As a result, Bernice tried to cope by writing everything down and having her supervisor repeat the directions. Because she could not trust herself to articulate her own questions and concerns, she tended to relate to her supervisor by letter, where she hoped that she could make her points in a less explosive way.

The stress was almost unbearable. Bernice describes coming to work with an incredible headache after Billy tore her hair off her head in a before-work attack on the street. Then she spent the day making sure she was accepted at work, pleasing her co-workers and her supervisor. If she said something that upset a co-worker, Bernice would vociferously apologize. "I was always trying to get forgiveness, to get accepted. I was always trying to be pleasing."

On the job one of Bernice's other problems was dealing with inappropriate anger. Since she was trying to work while being stalked, the terror remained buried inside but would come out inappropriately at work. When there was any kind of professional disagreement at the workplace, Bernice felt herself being attacked and consistently overreacted, to the extent that some of her colleagues called her paranoid. As a result, Bernice's overreaction became the issue, with everyone turning to blame Bernice, when the underlying problem, which caused the response, went unrecognized. This pattern became almost intolerable for Bernice.

Recently Bernice asked Jenny Wittner, the director of the Chicago Commons Employment Center, to give her impressions of Bernice as an employee during these early days. Jenny agrees that Bernice was so used to being on the defensive that she took everything on the job as an attack, even when nothing was really meant. "You directed every-thing at you. I think you were always looking for areas in which you needed to defend yourself."

Jenny further explains that Bernice did not know how to ask for what she needed without letting herself get angry and having it build up. "You have learned much better how to handle relationships with people at work; you have developed ways of asking for what you need and talking about things that bother you in an appropriate manner." Only when Bernice wrote Jenny a letter, setting out the problems she was having and making clear that Bernice wanted to improve the situation at work, did Jenny receive a new perspective on Bernice's situation. "That was the turning point, because in that letter you spoke about all these problems and you took responsibility for some of them and for changing. I was really impressed by that because it was the first time in this whole episode that any one had stopped blaming the other person and took some responsibility."

Subsequently, Jenny sent Bernice and her supervisor to special counseling made possible by the company's Employment Assistance Program (EAP). Jenny says that Bernice learned a great deal from that experience. "You were so excited when you got back from the EAP. I think it was a series of instructions of how to behave on the job, how to present yourself, how to take things not as personal things but as work things. After the counseling you were less personal and more professional. This created a big change in you at work, and your ses-sions were a part of it."

Bernice agrees about the value of the EAP sessions, where she says she learned for the first time how to be an employee. She says she primarily learned that on-the-job problems should be solved with facts, not emotions, and each employee has a responsibility to work coopera-tively to help solve problems at the workplace.

Observing the behavior of director Jenny Wittner has also served as a general education for Bernice over the years. "Jenny is all facts. She is not coming at problems with any emotion. I was all emotion. I started to watch her. She wants facts, she wants to rationalize things, she wants everyone to play a part in solving problems. That is how I picked up how to handle myself on the job."

Now, four years later, Bernice explains that she still has to rehearse how to engage her supervisor, who at times appears forbidding. "Can

78   we talk?" and "Do you have a few minutes?" are two approaches she
has practiced and used. To ensure that she presents herself appropriately
Bernice says she makes a written list of her points and sticks to them in
the meeting, unless she is asked a question. In fact, Bernice believes that
as a result of domestic violence she still has a tremendous communication problem. "I have trouble giving and receiving information. Maybe
there is a certain amount of emotion that takes away from the issue at
hand."

Bernice's problems on the job are not atypical. In a 1996 focus
group report conducted for the Missouri Department of Family Services, one case manager in Kansas City described the inappropriate responses of domestic violence victims in the workplace:

> They're either very passive, afraid to ask for what they need
> or want, or are afraid to show that they don't understand.
> Or they're very aggressive and approach it from the stand-
> point of, "Well, what's wrong with me? I did everything
> you said," but they lash out. They either totally withdraw
> or lash out, and as a result, they're unemployed or, in the
> case of education or training, they don't succeed.[5]

Anger has been identified as one of the major problems that survivors
of domestic violence must overcome. One domestic violence expert
believes that in order to cope daily with abuse, battered women cannot
fully recognize or reveal their anger to their partners lest they endanger
themselves. Once they have escaped the violent situation the depth of
the anger and rage they experience overwhelms them. The anger is
focused on two issues: the fact that the women were abused in the first
place, and their current, and less than ideal, circumstances. As women
learn more about domestic violence as part of a recovery process, they
understand the personal impact the domestic violence has had on them
and they feel angry. Anger "marks women's transition into believing
that they do not deserve to be abused and fully recognizing the extent
of the abuse they have suffered."[6]

But for anger to be channeled for positive purpose, it has to be
controlled, and it can be overwhelming. Like Bernice, women con-
sumed by anger can experience great difficulty in working coopera-
tively at the workplace. As it surfaces inappropriately at the work site

during the day, the anger simply can be too difficult for customers and co-workers to deal with. Only when Bernice had mastered and come to terms with her anger and depression could she become a valued, as opposed to a disruptive, employee. Luckily her supervisor was willing to give Bernice the time and offer her the assistance to learn how to productively channel her feelings at the workplace.

Recently, a Chicago domestic violence shelter hired Linda, a survivor of domestic violence and a longtime welfare recipient, to provide counseling and case management services to battered women in a demonstration program located in a welfare department office. Bernice, her case manager who was assisting her in her welfare-to-work journey, referred Linda for the job. A month later, Linda's arrival on the job was wrecking havoc. Reportedly Linda was constantly in aggressive battles and personality conflicts with co-workers, requiring continuous on-site counseling and group staff meetings on the part of the project's supervisor.

Bernice laughs when I inform her of the difficulties her protégé is encountering. "Linda has the exact same problem I had when I began work. She has never been an employee before. She doesn't realize that getting along with co-workers is part of her job." I ask what this has to do with being a victim of domestic violence. Bernice replies, "Everything. She isn't socialized. Linda has been so isolated. She has very few interpersonal skills, and they will have to be developed."

I'm not convinced. Linda's problem may be another aspect of domestic violence victimization that Bernice's experience illustrates. As a survivor of domestic violence who has received some therapeutic support, Linda is now terribly afraid of being revictimized. So now when she hears anything negative, Linda defends herself. As we have seen, Bernice's co-workers reported the same phenomenon. It could well be that the anger of former domestic violence victims as reported in the literature is more of a self-defense mechanism, in most instances a necessary hedge against further or repeat victimization. But regardless of the cause, at the workplace the response can be counterproductive.

Domestic violence survivors at work need to understand that negative feedback or corrective or constructive criticism at their job will occur on a daily basis, and if they are to remain employed they must be open to receiving it. Linda's supervisor understands but nonetheless

80   throws up her hands. "Who really has the time to deal with this on a daily basis?"[7]

A letter sent to me from Geraldine in Aberdeen, Washington, provides another example of how the fear of revictimization can affect domestic violence survivors at work. Although Geraldine has been out of her violent situation for two and a half years, a situation at work triggered the memories:

> One of the guys that I work with thought it was a big joke when he grabbed one arm and with his free hand slapped me hard on the back/shoulder blade area. Then shortly after that he grabbed my arm so hard that I was in tears. . . . He said he was only joking around. . . . Of course I talked to my boss and he saw the marks that were left and he was reprimanded for it. My question, though, is how can I get a better handle on these feelings?

In 1995 Geraldine was raped by two men, followed by an eight-month abusive relationship with a boyfriend. The scars remain open, making it difficult for Geraldine to function.

> When I got raped in 1995 by the two guys, I wished they had shot me with their gun because I would have rather been dead than have what happened to me happen. For three years after that I had to be tested for the HIV virus and for a week each time, all I could do was worry what the results were going to be. Though I am clear and don't have to be tested anymore, it still affects me because they took something from me.
>
> Every time I feel like someone is behind me I get real defensive and jumpy as though they are going to attack me. . . . The nightmares still to this day at times are so bad that I wake up in a cold sweat, looking around to see where he is at in the room and nobody is there. I don't feel safe unless I have a bat or something by my bed so I can defend myself. And this is in my parent's own house. If I am half-asleep and one of my parents comes upstairs in the dark, I am flying out of my bed, saying, "Don't hit me." Between the two situa-

tions I have had to go in for anger management courses
because my temper was so out of control.

Geraldine tells me that it is difficult to be nice to others because she is
frightened that if she is pleasant to people something bad is going to
happen over which she won't have any control.[8] In other words, battered women believe they simply can't afford to let down their guard.
This makes for aggressive employees who have great difficulties in the
workplace.

Sylvia Benson of STRIVE/Chicago Employment Service gives me a
graphic example of how domestic violence survivors struggle to cope
with the mental health effects of violence:

> We had gotten to that part of the workshop when we talk
> about the different things individuals have to do to initiate
> the employment search. The participant looked distraught
> and went into the washroom and started screaming. We per-
> suaded her to open the door. She screamed that she wanted
> to kill herself. There is no point in living, she couldn't do
> this anymore, it was too much. In her hand was a paper
> clip or a razor blade—something shiny. She told us that her
> partner was in jail for attempted robbery. He had been abu-
> sive to her, but now his relations were not supportive, blam-
> ing her for his arrest.
>
> Although she had been employed, she quit her job be-
> cause of the stress of this abuse from her relatives and went
> on welfare. She got trapped on welfare because her self-
> esteem had been destroyed through this process. Although
> public assistance served as a safety net for her and her
> daughter, she was unable to work herself out of it due to
> domestic violence. With the assistance of one week of in-
> patient hospital therapy and out-patient counseling, she now
> holds down two part-time cashier jobs and is off welfare.[9]

Several years ago I received a letter from Louise in Colorado Springs,
Colorado, who suffered severe physical abuse from her husband and
lost her job after thirteen years of employment as a warehouse supervisor because it became more and more obvious that "I wasn't quite all

82   together." Louise then went on welfare to support her children. In 1995 she became suicidal and spent a week at a mental institution where she began to receive medication and therapy. She now takes three psychotropic medications for her condition. The bruising and jarring of her brain along with eye injuries causes frequent and intolerable headaches. Louise writes:

> My life was fear, insecurity, confusion, uncertainty, worry, pain, and many days wishing I was dead. Life meant absolutely nothing, but another thing I had to do. Death becomes the final escape. You might say that I became the walking dead with no direction.
>
> In order to remain stable today, I think these things to myself (I do this all the time): In a time long ago, in a land far, far away, and tomorrow, and tomorrow and tomorrow. They help me to remember and survive. This is no fairy tale, although I wish it were. At least then, I could close the book.[10]

And here is a letter I received from another domestic violence survivor:

> I was a tenured professor on a research grant in Italy when I met my ex-husband. Within a few months, my productivity suffered significantly due to emotional turmoil, lack of sleep, and the demands he made upon the flexibility of my writing schedule. . . .
>
> When I returned to full-time teaching and took on the responsibility of department chair . . . he made things difficult for me professionally by such antics as abusing me all night before important meetings, making me late for meetings, intimidating me about conversing with male colleagues in my department, and even showing up at work unannounced. . . . Once he made me miss a meeting by closing the garage door before I was able to pull the car out and then threatening me with a can of gasoline until I turned the car off and talked to him for another hour. I fell substantially behind in my field, as I was first not able to pay atten-

tion at conference talks, then not even able to attend, and my ability to read professional literature started to deteriorate.

When I was finally successful at leaving him during our spring break, I was unable to return to work for the last seven weeks of classes due to fear of his stalking me and finding me (I stayed at friends in hiding for three months). My college had to hire a temporary replacement for me and still changed all the locks in the building since the secretary was terrified of my abuser, who, when I had tried to leave in the past, had gained access to the office and gone through my files. My ex-husband stole my computer, many of my research notes, and all my valuable family heirlooms. I developed severe posttraumatic stress disorder and was so obsessed with the courts and the police that I was unable to do any work for the next nine months. I had to renege on a book contract that I am still unable to complete.

I returned to work the next academic year, overriding my inner wisdom, due to fear of having no income, and started to deteriorate physically and psychologically. Soon I was having suicidal ideation; three months later, I was in bed every waking hour, except those I was teaching, due to environmental and food allergies, psychotropic drug reactions, and the exhaustion of being in a constant state of hyperarousal. I found a clinical psychologist willing to support my claim for temporary total disability.

I was off work for two years on disability, and then returned to teaching when I felt that my concentration and stamina had improved enough. But I soon found that I was not sufficiently recovered to handle the long hours and the stress. So I am off work again, still on SSI, and devoting myself full-time to my healing with great determination to recover and much hope.[11]

Mental health problems limit women's employment, and mental health effects of domestic violence certainly serve as significant barriers for some battered women. The psychologist Mary Ann Dutton usefully summarizes the recognized effects of domestic violence. These include

84   intrusion symptoms, or reexperiencing of the traumatic events; avoidance symptoms, which function to reduce awareness of the traumatic experience and its aftermath; anxiety; agoraphobic symptoms; sleep disturbance, difficulty concentrating, hypervigilance, physiological reactivity, and anger or rage, all of which share a common dimension of autonomic arousal; depression; grief; shame; lowered self-esteem; suicide ideation; suicide gestures or other self-destructive behavior; somatic complaints; use of alcohol and other addictive behaviors; and impaired functioning in occupational and other social roles. On another level, battered women can also be said to suffer from feelings of shame, self-blame, subjugation, morbid hatred, a sense of defilement, resignation or broken will, and revictimization, as well as feelings of bereavement, grief, and mourning.[12]

   Posttraumatic stress disorder is one way of systematizing some of the more serious psychological responses in women survivors of domestic violence. Developed first to measure the effects on males of war and heavy combat, posttraumatic stress disorder has only recently been shown to affect survivors of rape, domestic battering, and incest.[13] The posttraumatic stress disorder diagnosis is based on three categories of symptoms:[14]

> 1. Reliving or reexperiencing the trauma, dreaming about it, having flashbacks or feelings that the trauma is happening again, or being upset at events or experiences that remind the survivor of the trauma
>
> 2. Avoidance or numbing of responses, diminished interest in usual activities, feeling distant, having a sense of impending doom or not expecting to have a long life, career, or family
>
> 3. Increased arousal or hypervigilance as demonstrated by an inability to go to sleep or stay asleep, irritability, inability to concentrate, extreme watchfulness, or hair-trigger response

The consequences of posttraumatic stress disorder can fade and reemerge throughout a victim's lifespan. An example of this phenomenon came to my attention just today in an article in my morning newspaper, which reviewed the question of whether the Auschwitz survivor and prize-winning author Primo Levi killed himself in 1987, or whether his plunge down the stairwell of his Turin, Italy, apartment house was an accident. Circumstantial evidence that Auschwitz was haunting Levi was revealed two years ago when the chief rabbi of Rome stated that Levi had telephoned him ten minutes before he died. Although he did not mention suicide, Levi told the rabbi that he was depressed and couldn't go on with his life. Levi's mother was ill with cancer. Every time her son looked at her face, he would remember the faces of those men stretched on the benches at Auschwitz.[15]

The research literature on domestic violence finds abused women five times more likely to attempt suicide, fifteen times more likely to abuse alcohol, nine times more likely to abuse drugs, and three times more likely to be diagnosed as depressed or psychotic.[16] Some of the new research studies now give us some information about the extent of mental health problems experienced by women on welfare. Many of these mental health problems are likely to be effects of domestic violence but cannot be definitively proven without longitudinal data (which looks at whether these conditions are more likely to follow abuse) and multivariate analyses (which adjust for other differences between the abused and nonabused groups).

In the Worcester Family Research Project the lifetime prevalence of posttraumatic stress disorder for women in the combined sample was extremely high compared to the general population. Over one-third (about 35 percent) of all respondents met the criteria for lifetime post-traumatic stress disorder—three times the prevalence level among women in the general population. Fifteen and a half percent of housed mothers and 17.5 percent of homeless mothers were suffering from posttraumatic stress disorder at the time of the baseline interview. Almost 10 percent of the homeless, and almost 12 percent of the housed women, were currently experiencing a major depressive disorder. Nearly one-third of the homeless and over one-quarter of housed mothers reported that they had made at least one suicide attempt during their lifetime, typically before the age of eighteen years. Almost 55 percent of those who made suicide attempts made two or more.[17]

Women in the sample struggling with mental health issues had only half the odds of maintaining work as women without mental health problems, and those who had spoken to a clinician about mental health problems in the past six months had about one-third the odds of maintaining work. The study found that the mental health variables remained significantly and negatively associated with the capacity to maintain work, defined as thirty hours a week.[18]

Data from the University of Michigan's random sample of 753 women on welfare in an urban county of Michigan, research undertaken between April and December 1997, found an overrepresentation of battered women when mental health was screened. Those women who were violence victims within the last twelve months had nearly three times as many mental health problems as their nonabused counterparts; almost 62 percent qualified for a mental health diagnosis, and almost 37 percent for two or more diagnoses. Currently abused women were generally one and a half to two times more likely to have mental health problems than women who had been abused by their partners in their lifetime but not in the last year. Recent victims were also twice as likely to have received treatment for mental health problems than the past victims and the never-victimized group and twice as likely to report currently needing treatment than their counterparts who had experienced severe violence in their lifetime but not in the last twelve months.[19] When the various welfare-to-work barriers were correlated with the participants' ability to work twenty hours per week in the sample, women having a major depression were significantly less likely to work than those without the barrier.[20]

In Lisa Brush's sample of 122 welfare participants in Pittsburgh, one-third (34 percent) had at least one symptom from three posttraumatic stress disorder symptom categories (intrusion, constriction, and hyperarousal). Brush found that the traumatic stress symptom made a statistically significant difference in program participation outcomes. Women with trouble concentrating (an intrusion symptom) had similar dropout rates but significantly higher job placement rates than women not reporting that symptom. Those who reported angry outbursts (a symptom of hyperarousal) dropped out significantly more frequently than those who did not report hyperarousal. Brush tentatively concludes that some women with posttraumatic stress disorder are unable to work, but for others, work may ameliorate the symptoms.[21]

Although there is still not a great deal of research on this issue, it is likely that research will continue to implicate mental health issues in poor women's abilities to obtain or sustain employment, and it is important to remember that some of these mental health problems can be traced to the effects of violence. For the moment, it seems clearer than ever that not all battered women are alike, and they will continue to respond and struggle with varying degrees of resiliency to the effects of the abuse.

The research literature on domestic violence documents the fact that self-medication or numbing through alcohol or drugs is common among battered women.[22] The recent studies of domestic violence victims on welfare confirm these findings. The Worcester Family Research Project, for example, found that over one-third (about 38 percent) of all housed and homeless mothers met criteria for substance abuse or dependence at sometime during their life, compared to 18 percent of women in the general female population; 4 percent had had substance abuse or dependency problems within six months prior to the baseline study.[23]

Moreover, the study found that women who were long-term users of welfare were more likely to have a history of substance abuse or dependence during their lifetime. For example, long-term welfare users among the homeless were two times more likely to have a substance abuse problem than short-term users (61 percent compared to 31 percent); among the housed, long-term welfare users were approximately one and a half times more likely to abuse substances than short-term users (44 percent compared with 29 percent).[24]

Other recent samples found elevated problems with alcohol and drugs among currently abused women on welfare compared with women on welfare who were not abused. Within the sample of 846 women on welfare in Passaic County, New Jersey, surveyed between December 1995 and January 1997, 10 percent of the entire sample, and 19 percent of those currently abused within the sample, reported that they had a current problem with alcohol or drugs.[25] In the University of Michigan sample, abused women suffered eight times the amount of alcohol dependency of their never abused counterparts, and over three times the amount of drug dependency.[26] Overall, drug abuse significantly correlated with failure to work twenty hours a week.[27]

The implications of posttraumatic stress disorder and other trauma from violence for welfare and antipoverty policy are enormous. For the past five years, welfare policy has emphasized breaking the "culture of poverty" or "culture of dependency," a pattern of learned helplessness among the poor.[28] Given the extent to which girls and women on welfare have been or are victims of violence, we must incorporate knowledge of the effects of violence into antipoverty policy. It is likely that some of the helplessness observed is due to the effects of violence, not to the effects of poverty per se.

Rather than look at direct and indirect sabotage by intimate partners or to the effects of violence and trauma, researchers have attempted to find causes for this passivity within the girls and women themselves. For example, one antipoverty analyst identifies the problem that welfare recipients suffer as stemming from their lack of control; "learned helplessness" is the issue, a motivational deficit caused when one comes to believe that action is futile. And the cause of this "learned helplessness"? The repeated experience with lack of control or being labeled incompetent. This lack of control is deemed to be the result of living in poverty. "As a result, the environment and the perception of control or lack of control that the environment can induce have important consequences for behavior. . . . Repeated experience with uncontrollable life events in persistent poverty—such as unwanted pregnancies and discrimination—may interfere with one's ability to recognize new opportunities for advancement." Repeated experiences with lack of control or being labeled as incompetent make it less likely that people will recognize potentially effective actions later. For example, the woman who is repeatedly turned down in seeking a job is not likely to look for a job in the future. Fear of failure and lack of belief in personal control and efficacy are character failures induced by living in persistent poverty. Ultimately, someone who has been conditioned by a lack of control will not necessarily respond immediately to any new opportunities. As a result of these emotional deficits, one commentator believes that welfare policy must provide welfare recipients with voluntary choices as opposed to negative incentives.[29]

In a long and fairly influential discourse on the nonworking poor in America, Lawrence Mead carefully considers the theory of the "culture of poverty." He too finds many of the poor defeated. Mead describes a single mother on welfare in Boston who feels she cannot work because of the lack of child care, low wages, and other problems. For Mead it is obvious that this woman could find a job and could obtain child care through her state's workfare program. The point, however, is that she has a mentality that refuses to believe that opportunity exists even when it does. Concluding this anecdote, Mead states that as long as mothers like this have so little sense of freedom, no reforms in the labor market will do much to raise work levels. Policy, reasons Mead, must be addressed to these defeatist attitudes. "The poor will work more regularly if government enforces the work norm. Anti-poverty policies aimed at barriers or the self-interest of the poor have failed to raise work levels, while work requirements linked to welfare may succeed." Because of these reduced expectations of the poor, Mead says that government must expect—and require—work of its citizens.[30]

"Culture of poverty" proponents rightly identify lack of control as the issue but are unable to determine its cause. They look to cultural deficiencies of the women on welfare induced by the environment, rather than to the direct harmful actions of specific actors in that environment. In Bernice's case, it was not her cultural predisposition against work but the sabotage she experienced from a member of her household that undermined her efforts to enter the labor force. Because the research literature time and time again demonstrates the strong allegiance of low-income women to the prevailing cultural norms of work and the nuclear family, the issue of domestic violence seriously undercuts the viability of the "culture of poverty" concept.

Moreover, the similarities between "culture of poverty" behavior and the symptoms of posttraumatic stress disorder are startling. We have seen that the effects of sexual trauma and domestic violence include passivity, helplessness, and depression, all "culture of poverty" or "underclass" characteristics. As one trauma expert explains: "Incest victims tend to be extremely unassertive and passive, to the point of paralysis."[31]

Patricia Murphy, a vocational rehabilitation expert, has annotated the diagnostic criteria for posttraumatic stress disorder to relate the aspects of the disorder to possible vocational impairments. The themes of passivity, hostility, and helplessness expounded by the "culture of poverty" theorists permeate her analysis of the effects of trauma. For instance, recurrent and intrusive recollection of the battering event may lead to difficulty in learning and poor concentration; avoiding thoughts or feelings associated with the trauma may result in suppression of creativity, loss of confidence, and fear of new challenges; and a sense of a foreshortened future may lead to a feeling that planning is futile

90 and a predisposition against completion of classes and projects.[32] As one writer has expressed, when a person suffers from posttraumatic stress disorder, "the whole apparatus for concerted, coordinated, and purposeful activity is smashed."[33]

Also relevant to welfare policy is the relationship between low reading skills and domestic violence. Typically, domestic violence involves verbal and emotional abuse that may extensively hold back the intellectual development of abused women, who are told over and over that they are unintelligent or incompetent. Over time, the effects of this emotional abuse upon potential skills or vocational development may be more detrimental than the consequences of physical abuse. Patricia Murphy makes the useful point that many verbally abusive partners, who perceive that the development of good reading skills means that their partners will have access to information that is not screened and controlled by them, convince the women that they are not good readers.[34] In addition, these men understand that the development of skills will lead the women out of the house and into the labor market, a threatening step for them.

The correct characterization of the problem is critical, as the diagnosis will determine effective interventions. Because many domestic violence survivors need specialized interventions, proper diagnosis is required. When we are dealing with the effects of violence, such as low self-esteem, loss of confidence, or depression, it also becomes vital to properly assess the issue of violence lest only the symptoms of the problem and not its underlying cause be addressed. If, for example, drug or alcohol addiction is treated without attention to the underlying violence, a woman's coping mechanism may be removed, which may make the underlying situation worse for the woman, leaving her terrifyingly vulnerable to renewed memories or emotions. In addition, women whose depression is the result of domestic violence need to understand how being violence victims can cause them to suffer from both short- and long-term mental health problems. Understanding the cause of the depression gives women the knowledge and tools they need to successfully cope with this effect of domestic violence. Because some of the symptoms may fade over time but never entirely disappear, it is important for a domestic violence survivor to understand how the effects of violence will affect her, and how she can cope with them in her daily life.

⚜

Treatment to rebuild the smashed sense of self, to change critical ways of thought, and to build necessary confidence and self-esteem is required, and for some women the effort may well be a lifelong one. For one domestic violence survivor I interviewed, it took three years of consistent therapy and medication for her to overcome her agoraphobia, which developed after she left her abusing partner.[35]

What are the essential elements of the recovery process? The feminist author Carolyn Heilbrun writes, "Men tend to move on a fairly predictable path to achievement; women transform themselves only after an awakening. And that awakening is identifiable only in hindsight."[36] For trauma victims, the awakening begins as the victim leaves the abuser, but the transformation process is just beginning.

Without recapitulating the contents of the entire recovery literature, for policy purposes it is important for us to understand the basic features of the recovery process. The first step involves establishing safety. Second, it is important to explore the trauma, through narrating and to a certain extent reliving the traumatic experiences in an attempt to fill out available memories and access previously repressed ones. Then the focus shifts to putting to use the understanding the survivor gains from the narrative, to build self-esteem, to find a way to go on with one's life that acknowledges and integrates the reality of the trauma, and to mobilize resources for the new tasks ahead.[37]

Education of the survivor is the key. Professionals emphasize that transformation of the trauma may be a lifelong process for the survivor. Informing survivors about typical posttraumatic reactions can normalize those responses for battered women and help them develop personal coping skills, as well as a greater sense of self-efficacy or empowerment.[38] Recognizing that her abusive situation is part of a larger social problem also helps to create a different perspective from which the survivor of domestic violence may go forward. Women who have been taught that their role is to be supportive, helpful, and loving to their partner will often respond to domestic violence by internalizing the failure; they most often look into their own behavior as an exploration of male aggression. They think, perhaps, that they provoked the situation or that somehow they weren't giving enough.[39] I remember Bernice telling me with great excitement that she learned while in support

92   group in shelter that she was a battered woman—one of many. As this knowledge removed the sense of personal blame and shame she had been shouldering for years, it marked a liberating moment.

Most people who are being abused are not knowledgeable. They feel that the abuse is something unique that has happened only in their relationship. But when they learn that the same cycle is happening to just about every woman who is involved, abuse victims start to look at the events differently, less personally. When one thinks of the isolation in which many poor girls and women live and the fact that the majority never receive any personal attention or assistance in dealing with the effects of sexual or physical abuse, one realizes the extent to which they have been denied the critical knowledge and information they need to understand what has happened to them and to make use of these insights to move ahead in a positive way.

For battered women to be able to protect themselves and escape abusive situations, challenging socialized beliefs about sex roles may also be required. Experts believe that women whose sex role attitudes are more traditional may be at greater risk once the abuse occurs. "Holding to the beliefs that a woman is responsible for her partner's happiness, that she is obligated to provide herself as a willing sexual partner at his demand, or that major decisions must be approved by the man who is head of household may reduce the battered woman's options for escape or avoidance of abuse." A traditional sex role belief may even mandate that a woman tolerate physical and sexual force.[40] Carolyn Heilbrun's depiction of rigidly determined sex roles accurately captures the essence of relationships that are violent. The girl does not become an individual but puts a man at the center of her life. "The young woman died as a subject, ceased as an entity. The boy defines himself as 'not woman.' "[41] Lori Heise, an international expert on women's health, explains that ethnographic descriptions of societies that have little or no violence against women are striking in their lack of strongly defined gender roles. Citing McConahay and McConahay's study of seventeen cultures, she postulates that "gender-role rigidity is highly correlated with interspousal violence."[42]

James Gilligan's many years of work with violent incarcerated men also leads him to focus on sex role stereotyping as the factor creating the differences between men's use of violence and women's becoming victims of violence:

Women, by contrast, have traditionally been taught that they will be honored if, and only if, they accept a role that restricts them to the relatively passive aim of arranging to be loved by men and to depend on men for their social and economic status, forgoing or severely limiting or disguising activity, ambition, independence, and initiative of their own. This set of injunctions decreases women's vulnerability to behaving violently, but it also inhibits women from participating actively or directly in the building of civilization, in part by reducing them to the role of men's sex objects.[43]

Most Americans are firmly attached to traditional roles for women. In an international Gallup poll involving twenty-two nations, nearly half of the Americans surveyed said the ideal family structure was one in which only the father earned the living and the mother stayed home with the children, compared with only about one-fourth of those polled in Germany, India, Lithuania, Spain, Taiwan, and Thailand.[44] And in a recent *Washington Post* poll, 69 percent of the men and 68 percent of the women surveyed agreed with the following proposition: "It may be necessary for mothers to be working because the family needs the money, but it would be better if she could stay home and just take care of the house and children."[45]

For women of color in the United States, now representing the majority of the women on welfare, response to the issue of gender roles is more complex. Kimberle Crenshaw describes the world of limited or constricted responses of black women: for example, women of color are reluctant to call the police, "a hesitancy likely due to a general unwillingness among people of color to subject their private lives to the scrutiny and control of a police force that is frequently hostile. There is also a more generalized community ethic against public intervention, the product of a desire to create a private world free from the diverse assaults on the public lives of racially subordinated people."[46] Most of the African American women Beth Richie interviewed strongly desired a traditional nuclear family because they believed in their predestined role to support a black man. Here is Lynne, age twenty-eight, detained on a drug charge:

> I remember wanting a kind, sweet husband when I grew
> up; someone who I could reach out for my dreams with,
> just the two of us. It would be very different from my
> mother and father. I wanted more romance, intimacy, and
> affection. A fuller, more loving life. He'd be in charge and
> I'd follow his lead. I was a kingmaker at heart. It was my life
> dream to support a strong man.[47]

Jill Nelson also agrees that, as a reaction to slavery, black women see
that one of the functions of the postslavery black community, and black
women in particular, has been the restoration of black manhood. "Our
job became to make black men feel like men by making sure we didn't
dominate, intimidate, or, like ol' Massa, emasculate." Black women
have some mistaken notion that standing up against sexism in all its
forms constitutes being disloyal to black men.[48] By protecting men of
color from further racial stigmatization, battered women of color can
be said to collude with their partners' violence.[49]

Two other social analysts posit a slightly different reason for black
women's adherence to traditional sexually defined roles. The Chicago
Tribune columnist Clarence Page argues that many black women worked
to secure for themselves the very home-centered role against which
some white women rebelled. "Instead of struggling to get out of traditional home roles and into the workplace, black women dreamed, more
often than not, of escaping the workplace and enjoying the luxury of
spending more time at home."[50] bell hooks too argues that for black
women the family is a basis of solidarity and resistance to white racism
and that for women of color the work available to them is drudgery.
For this reason, hooks has been resistant to white feminists' advocacy
of paid work as a solution to the powerlessness of housewives. Wrested
from their husbands and children during slavery, when family members faced being auctioned off to different masters, African American
women never had the opportunity to enjoy the Victorian norm of female domesticity.[51]

Even those women who work cling to traditional gender roles. Richie notes that for the African American women in her study, the harder
they worked outside the home, the more strongly they held to their
fantasies of traditional gender roles and domestic arrangements, which
included giving the man the dominant role in the family. Richie argues

that commitment to traditional gender roles led the women to entrapment in domestic violence.[52]

Having chosen traditional sex roles, many battered women have not formed a vocational self-concept. Although we know that domestic violence interferes with the development of self-esteem, critical for vocational success, lack of a vocational self-concept is another major barrier. Many battered women have delayed vocational development. At the time that they should have been developing a vocational identity—a sense of their strengths and occupational interests—they were devoting themselves to their partners and raising their children. Patricia Murphy explains that this delayed vocational development makes it difficult for battered women to successfully enter the labor market:

> Russell has named the ages between thirteen and twenty-six years the statistically vulnerable years for marital rape, stranger rape, acquaintance rape, inducement and exhortation into prostitution. These years correspond to the prime vocational identity development years for most girls and young women. That is, most girls and young women are completing their education and entering the labor market during these years. For PTSD [posttraumatic stress disorder] survivors who have these experiences in their background as well as the experience of domestic violence, the demand that they select a vocational goal and pursue it may be incomprehensible or impossible for them. This is because work identity formation and development may have been impaired during these critical years. Such women have deeply rooted PTSD symptoms and may need prolonged vocational exploration before they can settle into a vocational direction. Vocational exploration is part of work identity formation and usually takes place in formal educational settings and by trying out part-time, summer, and full-time jobs.
>
> In my vocational expert witness testimony practice, I have found extensive (six months to a year) vocational exploration to be needed for newly divorced women who married very early and found themselves in an abusive relationship from their youngest adult years onward.[53]

96   Certainly, many women on welfare who have never worked and who have lived in persistent poverty lack this basic vocational self-concept. Low-income battered women, however, having been even more isolated by their partners, have even more serious problems with self-worth, and hence have even more difficulty developing a vocational self-concept.

In comparative terms, abused women need greater support than do typical female clients in understanding and accepting their potential and abilities and in recognizing their strengths. In helping these women achieve such goals, the tasks of the counselor become very complex and include using appropriate role models in group counseling to enhance the sense of competence and acceptance among abused women. Abused women may be able to accept superficially that they are people of worth, but it takes positive experiences over time for them to internalize this concept.[54]

As she was beginning her first job, Bernice was addressing many of these issues while wrestling with basic safety concerns because of the stalking. In hindsight it is clear that Bernice was suffering from post-traumatic stress disorder symptoms, including flashbacks, nightmares, sleeplessness, and depression. She never received help from a professional trauma expert who might have helped her to cope with these lingering effects of the violence. That many women should give up work when faced with such problems is not surprising. Had Bernice had effective counseling and support during this process, might her recovery from the effects of the violence been swifter and her experience less overwhelming?

Unfortunately, just when Bernice was making progress on all these fronts, a new development occurred that set back her recovery.

CHAPTER SIX

Little Billy's Dilemma

> I walk over the marsh saying, I am I; & must follow that
> furrow, not copy another. That is the only justification for
> my writing & living.
>
> —VIRGINIA WOOLF, *The Diary of Virginia Woolf*

Bernice had just come home from work when the doorbell rang. When she went downstairs she saw it was a sheriff's officer, who handed her an envelope. She wanted to open it but at the same time was afraid that something had gone wrong with someone in the family.

When Bernice finally had the courage to open and read the papers, she saw that Billy was filing for legal custody of eleven-year-old Little Billy. It was a *pro se* petition, filed by Billy himself, with many misspelled words, but Bernice knew it was nevertheless a legal document that she had to take seriously.

When she spoke to Little Billy, he confirmed that he did want to live with his father. He told Bernice that it would mean that he would have his dad back, even if he had to share him with his new family—Billy was in a new relationship. Little Billy told Bernice that it would be like "we were before." He said he felt he needed to be raised by a man. "I need that manly thing, you know, that male bonding."

After all she had risked to provide her son with a safe environment, Bernice was crushed that Little Billy now wanted to live with his father. Bernice felt betrayed. She believed that Billy had manipulated Little Billy, and she determined to fight back.

She spoke with Billy outside after she had dropped Little Billy off at his father's apartment for a visit. Billy proposed an even split of the children and promised it would buy peace between them.

> I said, "No, we are going to have to fight then." He said, "Okay, let's start right now." And at that moment I got really afraid and all those feelings started to come back. I felt so trapped. I ran to my car and drove away.

Later, however, Bernice decided she did not want to fight anymore. As all the feelings started to rush back, she realized that she no longer wanted to deal with the darkness that was again descending.

> I was really hurt. I was hurt because I had gotten Little Billy away from domestic violence and he was pulling us back in.

Bernice realized that she would have to deal with Billy again and there would be the usual manipulation, blackmail, and other emotional abuse. But she couldn't enter that battlefield again.

> I didn't fight him, because the kids wanted the fighting to stop. So I signed the papers. I figured that if I gave him custody, the fighting would really stop, and it has. But I had to give up my son to get this.

Bernice hoped that if she gave up something, that if Billy got a "win over her," he would drop the anger and bitterness and leave her alone.

Moreover, Little Billy really wanted to go live with his father, and if Bernice didn't give in, she believed, then her own son would resent her. To win the right to go to his father's, Little Billy waged an effective campaign. He acted up, he talked back, he was completely obnoxious, and he got in trouble. Bernice was sure that Little Billy would run away from her house if she didn't let him go.

> I felt my back was up against the wall. It made me cry because it made me sad. Little Billy thought life with his father was going to be one way when I knew it was going to be another. The fact was that I really couldn't protect my son from his own fantasies without

making him resent me. My son was so innocent and he just didn't
know.

Complicating the situation was the fact that Billy was in a live-in relationship with a woman on welfare with three children, and Bernice
knew that the relationship was violent. Once again, Little Billy would
be back in an environment in which he would be viewing domestic
violence on a daily basis.

> He is back in the same environment as I left. He has walked right
> back into it. I felt like I had given up, that I thought about my needs
> rather than my son's. I wasn't being a good parent. I was sacrificing
> Little Billy's life because I didn't have the strength to fight Billy and
> deal with my son's fantasies.

Yet the loving relationship with her own son would have been threatened—and perhaps totally ruptured—had Bernice fought Billy's custody petition. For Bernice, both now and then, her relationship with
her son is her first priority.

For this reason, Bernice is pretty sure she's in denial about how
observing domestic violence is affecting her son. Because she can't
change the situation and it would be dangerous for her to interfere, she
simply can't think about it.

> People might say, that is your child over there, you should have more
> feeling about it, but I don't. I don't know why. I almost feel cold on
> the inside when I think about it. Little Billy understands more, he
> doesn't have to be a part of it to a certain extent. I advise him to go
> to his room and close the door, and if it gets too bad, to go to a
> telephone booth and call me and I'll come and get him.

When Little Billy left, Bernice says, she was lost. Little Billy was a big
part of her life, and his not being there saddened her. Yet there was
relief as well.

> I didn't know if this boy was going to hurt himself or hurt someone
> else. So when he did leave there was upset on the one hand, and on

the other side there was relief. Maybe my son wouldn't act up and
do bad things if he were with his father.

Still, Bernice's decision to capitulate sent her reeling.

> The insomnia, the night sweats, it all came back after the custody
> thing. I couldn't sleep. I was constantly watching Jessica, getting up
> at night, I was locking doors. The nightmares, they seemed so real.
> He was always trying to kill me and hurt me, and I was always
> running. When I woke up my whole nightgown and where I lay in
> bed would be completely wet. I would wake up and my heart would
> be beating and I could not sleep for the rest of the night. I would sit
> up and smoke a whole pack of cigarettes.

At work Bernice couldn't focus. She tried to throw herself into her job,
to keep busy.

> You try not to communicate with people because you don't want
> them to see the tears in your eyes. So I hid it, like I have so many
> things from my job.

For Jessica, Little Billy's decision was a major relief. Bernice thinks that
Jessica was glad it didn't have to be her. She implicitly understands that
since her father chose Little Billy, she is free to remain with her mother.
"When Jessica felt she really didn't have to go, she was really relieved,"
explains Bernice, "but she was really sad for Little Billy." Although
Jessica cried after Little Billy left and was lonely, she gradually began to
rebuild her life by making new friends.

Under the custody arrangement, Little Billy is supposed to come to
Bernice one weekend a month. Although the custody agreement re-
quires that Billy transport his son to therapy every other week, Billy
stopped bringing him after three visits. Instead, Bernice enrolled Little
Billy in an after-school program in which the boy participates in basketball and leadership development activities several times a week. Bernice
has made it her business to let Little Billy's counselor know that the boy
is living in a home in which domestic violence is a daily occurrence.
Recently Billy has agreed that if Bernice pays for it and picks up Little

Billy each morning, he will allow him to go to camp this summer with his little sister.

Many months later, Bernice no longer felt guilty about her decision. The children's therapists have convinced her not to feel culpable about releasing her son if it makes her safe and if it gives Jessica the stability and secure home that she needs.

A year ago, at my request Bernice took Little Billy back to his therapist without Billy's knowing about it. Afterward, the therapist told Bernice that her son informed him that he would now rather be with his mother. The twelve-year-old was in a real crisis. He wants to come home, but he knows that his father isn't going to let him. If Little Billy were to express his real needs and interests, he could put himself as well as his mother and sister in real jeopardy. Understanding this, the boy has pretty much given up the idea of returning to Bernice's home. Bernice has no answer for Little Billy's problem. And now her son is cut off from therapy, which would at least give him a chance to verbalize his feelings and fears, instead of bottling them up.

So now, several years later, Little Billy understands what Bernice realized he didn't know when he made his critical decision. What is Little Billy's life like with his father?

> I think his life is very confusing. He's very isolated and he is very lonely. I don't think there is good dialogue. His dad lets him stay out quite late and I understand that Little Billy takes full advantage of the opportunity. He's not there a lot. He has talked to me about running away from his dad's house, and I have told him that I would get in trouble if I kept him here. He says he just wants to run away and live somewhere else.

Bernice understands full well that her son, just as he is becoming an adolescent, already a time of conflict and stress, is in an especially bad place. Little Billy knows his father loves him, but his father simply can't give him the personal attention he needs. Little Billy is afraid to express his needs because he understands that the answer is going to be no. Instead of being turned down, he doesn't talk, and he stays away from certain subjects that he knows upset his dad. Anything that concerns attention, love, or money—these are the things that upset him. Billy goes to work and gives attention to his girlfriend. Little Billy is in the middle, and he says he feels left out. And when the arguing starts, the clouds descend.

> He lives in such a chaotic state. He doesn't have peace in his life.
> My son was more talkative than he is now. He is quiet, and when
> he talks he talks really low. I can see some of my own behavior
> patterns that I had, the quietness. He has to force himself to be
> relaxed, to have a good time, as though there is something wrong
> with having a good time. He withdraws from people. These are a lot
> of the behavioral traits that I had. Although he is not the one being
> physically abused, I think that all the kids in the household pick up
> these behaviors.

Billy doesn't always let Bernice have Little Billy the one weekend a month the court ordered. Recently, he punished Bernice because the IRS has caught him in a tax fraud. When Bernice's tax refund was held up because the IRS found that Billy had also claimed to have custody of the children in previous years, Bernice was able to prove to the IRS that she had the children during the years in question, which left Billy holding the bag.[1]

Now, when Little Billy is permitted to visit Bernice, he wants to stay. Sometimes he locks himself in his room at Bernice's apartment and cries. But when it is time to drive home on Sunday night, he is very quiet. Bernice says she leaves him in peace during the drive.

> I don't really bother him. I try to give him the reassurance that I
> love him, that I'm not angry with him, that we're still family. On
> the drive home I always let him know, I'll keep coming back. Like
> in the AA group meetings, "I'll keep coming back." He keeps telling
> that to me. I feel really good that we have our own special wording
> and language that we use with one another.

This past summer Bernice got Little Billy a job as camp counselor and transported him to work in the morning and picked him up in the evening. She took him to the bank to cash his check and drove him so he could shop with his money. Because she saw him on a daily basis in the summer, at least, Bernice believed that she was able to give Little Billy the sense that his mother is involved in his daily life. Once school started again, maintaining that sense became more difficult, but she will continue to do little things like buying him clothes and uniforms and taking him to the doctor.

Bernice says that Little Billy will never confront his father and tell him he wants to go home to his mother. He knows that would bring about a large fight and a really chaotic situation. Little Billy won't go that far. But he will continue to walk around and feel bad about his life.

So Bernice may have made the right choice after all. Throughout the process her aim has been to maintain the love and respect of her son. That was the real reason for her decision, for had her son not wanted to live with his father, Bernice might have found the courage and strength somewhere to fight Billy yet again.

Bernice tells me that her motivation was made clear to her when she analyzed a new dream she had recently. For years her dreams all involved Billy's running after her and chasing her. Now the dreams are different. Bernice dreamed that Billy was abusing her and after she pressed charges against him he got ten years in jail.

> I had to go over to Billy's house to get Little Billy and bring him home because of the prison time. The hostility from Little Billy was tremendous. He was throwing stuff at me. He hated me. These are the types of dreams that I have now—Little Billy hates me for taking him away from his dad.

Bernice doesn't believe that Little Billy really wants to come home.

> It's just emotions—it comes and goes. I think that Little Billy has the hope that his dad is going to change. I understand that. It is like a woman living in domestic violence. That is something that you can't take away from a woman. She believes that her husband is going to change. And as long as he thinks that his dad is going to change, he needs to remain. Little Billy hasn't gotten old enough to realize that his dad is not going to change. And until he realizes these things, he has many more challenges to face. I'm not going to interrupt the course he has to go down. I'm going to let him go. I don't force anything. I just try to do what I can do and what I can't I give to God and I keep going.

104   Because one weekend a month isn't enough time for Bernice, she has devised different methods to be with her son and maintain communication with him. Bernice works overtime to stay involved in his life. Because she doesn't have legal custody, Little Billy's school report card can't be released to her. His teacher kindly calls Bernice on the telephone at work to discuss Billy's school progress. Bernice comes to Little Billy's classroom to participate in activities, and she also stops by the school to watch her son play basketball in the after-school program.

Billy doesn't get home from work until six-thirty in the evening. Bernice now begins work at seven-thirty in the morning, which enables her to drive over to Billy's apartment after her workday has ended and before Billy gets home from work.

> Sometimes I just go over and sit in the car in front of the apartment and listen to music on the car radio. Little Billy comes out and sits with me in the car. I take him clothing and bring him little care packages. Sometimes we will go to the music store and I will buy him something new, and we sit in the car just listening to the music. Or we go out and eat hamburgers together. We stay together for about forty-five minutes. Billy just doesn't know about it.

CHAPTER SEVEN

The Single Mother Myth and the Role of Welfare and Work

Very little is known about women.

—VIRGINIA WOOLF, *in a draft of* A Room of One's Own

The official story goes like this: In 1970 single mothers headed 48 percent of poor families with children. By 1993 single mothers headed 60 percent of poor families with children. Well over one-fifth of today's children live in families whose income is below the poverty line. Over half (57 percent) of these children reside in single-mother-headed families.[1]

New data about the prevalence of domestic violence cast considerable doubt about the validity of this picture. In light of the data about domestic violence and welfare, it is apparent that researchers and statisticians have and continue to confuse marriage with cohabitation. The presence of abusers in the lives of large percentages of women on welfare means that we need to seriously rethink conventional wisdom about the large number of single mothers supposedly raising their children without the presence of a male.

Interestingly, three researchers' random samples have provided us with our own "unofficial" census. Susan Lloyd's neighborhood survey finds that 71 percent of the entire sample of 824 women in one low-income Chicago neighborhood were in a relationship with a man at the time of the interview. Of these in a relationship, almost 70 percent lived with their partner. Very few women in the sample actually lived alone (5.6 percent). Of those on public assistance within the last twelve months, 63 percent stated they were in a relationship with a man considered their boyfriend. According to Lloyd, 52 percent of those in such a relationship stated that they lived with the male partner.[2]

Bill Curcio's New Jersey study found a similar proportion, with 66 percent of his sample of welfare recipients currently in a relationship with a man.[3] And according to Lisa Brush, 55 percent of the 114 women who answered the question said they were currently in a relationship. Of those sixty-three women, 27 percent said the relationship was casual or dating, 43 percent said it was serious, and 29 percent said they were living together or engaged. Thus, 72 percent of the women who were in a relationship stated it was serious.[4]

These new "census" data forces us to abandon two concepts—the deadbeat dad and the irresponsible single mother. Let's briefly examine each of these mythological constructs.

First, the deadbeat dad. Researchers and advocates focusing on the disappearance of the father in American families are dramatic in their depiction of the situation. Three examples should suffice to illustrate their picture of a world without men. Here is William Bennett in testimony before the U.S. House of Representatives, speaking about the problem of the female-headed household:

> When I was Drug Czar . . . whenever I went to a city—and I went to 105 cities—I would ask to be taken to the worst place. The place I almost always ended up was public housing. There was the world . . . a place of women and children. There were no men there . . . the only men around on a daily basis were the drug predators who were waiting to make their easy hits.[5]

David Blankenhorn, the founder and president of the Institute for American Values, lays out the statistics showing that in the 1990 census more than 36 percent of all children in the United States were living apart from their fathers, more than double the rate in 1960:

> The new conditions, driven by divorce and out-of-wedlock childbearing, split the nucleus of the nuclear family. Now

the father is physically absent. When he comes "home," his children are not there. He is not a husband. Because the parental alliance has either ended or never begun, the mother has little reason or opportunity to defend or even care about his fatherhood. In the most important areas, he is not responsible for his children.[6]

And David Popenoe, a professor of sociology at Rutgers University:

> Fatherlessness caused by nonmarital births now virtually equals that caused by divorce, and its effects on children have been shown to be even more deleterious than divorce on children's lives. In most divorce situations, children at least have had the advantage of a father's presence for part of their lives. For the majority of children born out of wedlock, the father is out of the picture from the very beginning.[7]

The overgeneralized picture presented is monolithic and extreme: poor men have in the majority of cases gone AWOL on their families. Nor is the picture any different as depicted by influential commentators on the women's side. Low-income women are the downtrodden heroines, heroically raising their children on their own in conditions of unspeakable poverty. Because some feminists and social policy analysts believe that most women on welfare are living without a man and raising their children on their own, it is incumbent upon them to explain why so many girls and women do so.

Responding to the demonization of these women, one well-known writer points the finger at the missing men who seduce and abandon the women:

> The role of males in forcing or persuading young women to have sex, in refusing to use condoms, in discouraging women from using other kinds of birth control, and in walking away from their responsibilities once their partners become pregnant has barely been addressed by politicians and many social policy experts.
>
> What "welfare reform" really means is that women are

being forced to take on both roles full-time without either adequate salaries or adequate help in providing for their children. Many mothers must provide care and love and food and clothing and values and discipline while holding down a full-time job and earning wages either below or close to the poverty line. They are increasingly expected to do all this both without the help of a man, since many of the men are nowhere to be found, and without the help of the society.[8]

The fault of this analysis, and others like it, lies in the overgeneralizations made about the women and their living arrangements; the description fits some, but not all, unmarried mothers. As we have seen, many of these women are in no way abandoned by these men, but instead find it rather difficult to rid themselves of them. Advocacy of a federalized welfare system for single mothers, providing an adequate cash benefit above the poverty line, as advocated by some of these commentators, could prove to make these girls and women even more prone to being controlled by their partners; the men might be attracted by the higher benefits, as well as by the fact that these women are not in the labor market and can be more readily kept within their sphere.

Other experts present a less passive picture of single mothers who have voluntarily chosen single motherhood. The reasoning goes as follows: More women are choosing to be single mothers as the social stigma associated with unwed mothers has declined. Given the high rates of sexual and physical abuse, these women may be much better off having chosen voluntarily to live apart from boyfriends or ex-husbands. "The rising number of single mothers suggests that more and more women have decided 'I'm better off without him,' even if it means being a single parent."[9]

This conclusion, based on official census statistics, confuses marriage and cohabitation, a common error in the antipoverty debate. But more importantly, this analysis, and others like it, makes assumptions about all single mothers. As a result of Bernice's story and the fast-accumulating data, we have seen that many poor young women may not be choosing motherhood but instead may be victims of unprotected or coerced sex. Like Bernice, they may not be rational agents, empowered and free to make choices and decisions for themselves, but are motivated by deep confusion and even fear. If this is the case for many girls and women, policy experts should not so blithely accept single parenthood as just a fact of life for our times. Even though conservatives have made this a hot topic, the issue of domestic violence should force everyone to take a good second look at the issue of single motherhood.

Demonstrating that Bernice's story is not atypical, recent data are beginning to paint a new and more nuanced picture of men's and women's living arrangements. Newly published data analysis from the National Maternal and Infant Health Survey provides us with some tantalizing clues. The survey, conducted by the National Center for Health Statistics from 1988 to 1991, is a nationally representative sample of women ages fifteen through forty-nine who had a live birth, fetal death, or infant death in 1988. Among mothers aged fifteen through seventeen who had a child in 1988, 27 percent had a partner at least five years older than themselves. The youngest mothers were the most likely to have a partner five or more years older. Moreover, childbearing occurs within the context of ongoing close relationships for a large portion of the fifteen- to seventeen-year-old mothers who have older partners. Thirty-five percent of the girls with older partners had been cohabiting during the pregnancy, and 49 percent were living with their partner at the time of the interview, held up to thirty months after the birth. Researchers found that mothers with an older partner were significantly more likely than those with a similar age partner to have cohabited during the pregnancy and to be doing so at the time of the interview. For younger mothers at least, cohabitation occurred in about half the relationships.[10]

Yet another data set provides new information about cohabitation patterns. Using data from the 1979–86 rounds of the National Longitudinal Survey of Labor Market Experience of Youth, a nationally representative sample of 12,686 men and women between the ages of fourteen and twenty-one, Frank Mott studied the presence of males in the homes of children born to women between the ages of fourteen and twenty-five, as well as those homes in which there were children under the age of four at the 1986 survey date. Researchers found that overall statistics about absent fathers mask large numbers of children who either had potentially important substitute fathers available or significant continuing contact with their biological father. For example, for older children, approximately 64 percent were living with their

110   biological father as of the 1986 survey. An additional 9 percent had an
absent biological father whom they saw at least once (and frequently
more times) a week. There were a remaining 26 percent who had less
contact with their biological father.

Of this latter group, 7 percent were living with their mother's new
spouse or partner whom the mother considered as a father figure. Thus,
a minimum of 80 percent of the children studied were residing in
situations in which they had substantial contact with male figures. "Traditionally used statistics on father presence or absence may substantially
misrepresent the reality of meaningful father or father-figure contact,
particularly for black children."[11] Importantly, the analysis challenges
analytical frameworks that accept a single common scenario of a parent
present, followed by family breakdown and the father's absence from
the home.

Two-thirds of the welfare program enrollees in Lisa Brush's sample
still saw the fathers of their children in some capacity, and 21 percent
lived with the father of one of their children. More than half (58 percent) said they received cash or gifts from the fathers of their children,
and over a third (34 percent) reported that they received formal child
support payments.[12]

In her researches in Harlem, Katherine Newman also found that "it
would be drawing too broad a brush stroke to suggest that men have
absented themselves wholesale from the inner city." Uncles, fathers,
brothers, sons, boyfriends, and husbands are very much in evidence,
she says; they help to support the households they live in and provide
support to the mothers of their children with whom they may not live.
"The Bureau of the Census or a sociologist looking at a survey could
easily miss the presence of men in Harlem households where they do
not officially live, but to which they are nonetheless important as providers."[13]

One economist colleague has asked me whether it is important to
determine whether these men actually live with the women. And why
does it matter if we call these women single mothers or not? I submit
that it very much matters that we get it right. If the relationship is live-
in, if it is long-term, if the male is the father of one or more of the
children, and if the relationship is violent, qualitative research has demonstrated that escape from the relationship can be extremely difficult.
The longer the relationship and the longer the duration of the violence,

then the more isolated the woman becomes, and the fewer resources and support networks she will have available to her. Although the violence or sabotage may be the same, the ability to escape may be totally different for the woman in a live-in relationship. And the longer the relationship, the more the woman has invested in it, which also appears to limit her choices.

✤

This new information about the high percentages of low-income women who are in relationships with men also calls into question the conceptualization of welfare as an important safety net so that women need not depend on men. Some American feminists have chosen to view the program in this way: "These women do not construct their lives as half of a male-breadwinner, female-homemaker pair, but rather they see their roles as *single* mothers as central to their lives"[14] Or, in the words of another, the welfare program became controversial when it became apparent that women were being provided benefits "even as they were violating the rules of patriarchy."[15] The availability of benefits means that women do not need to become involved in the traditional family arrangements held so sacred by conservatives; this conceptualization squarely pits some feminists against the nuclear family proponents and the religious right.

When applying their patriarchal theories to welfare policy, some feminists advocate more adequate benefits to enable poor mothers to stay at home to care for their children. "Single motherhood as a social phenomenon should be viewed by feminists as a practice resistive to patriarchal ideology, particularly because it represents a 'deliberate choice' in a world with birth control and abortion. As such, the existence of single motherhood as an ever-expanding practice threatens the logic and hold of the dominant ideology."[16]

These writers view single motherhood as a matter of deliberate choice for all single mothers, a view unsupported by research literature. As the research continues to demonstrate that many low-income girls and women have embraced the ideal of the nuclear family and their gendered role with it, it is important to discard a view of welfare as one that assists women in remaining independent of men. Instead, we need to shift our attention to how this vital safety net of welfare can also serve to trap women into hooking up with and remaining with abusive men.

What, then, does qualitative research tell us about the role of welfare benefits in this story? We have seen that for many low-income girls, the longing for their own nuclear family and the idealization of their own gendered role within such a unit causes them to form partnerships with men at early ages. For some, like Bernice, for whom earlier sexual assaults and abuse cause them to yearn for more functional families of their own, these partnerships appear at the time to meet their developmental needs for love and belonging. The existence of welfare programs does not appear to play much of a role in these life decisions. Although many low-income women on welfare cannot subsist on welfare benefits alone and may gravitate toward men who can help support them, the likely motivation is not economic support but love and belonging.

Welfare, however, can play a later trapping role. Because they have not developed their skills, a vocational identity, or any work experience, and because the world of work thus remains alien to them, some women on welfare find their choices limited when they realize that it is time to escape the abusive relationship. Welfare benefits alone are also too low in the United States to enable women to have the economic wherewithal to escape violence and support themselves and their children.

In addition to limiting the economic resources available, welfare receipt constrains the many women on welfare who believe that they cannot pursue help from normal channels that, although at best weak, are available for many women. Many women on welfare are afraid that if they interact with the government they might lose their welfare benefits (because of the illegal man in the house) or lose their children, who have been viewing domestic violence, to the child protective agency. As a result of welfare usage, battered women say that abusive partners may be in a more powerful position within low-income communities because they know the women will not complain or report them to anyone.[17]

There may yet be another role that welfare plays. Abusers, Bernice says, are attracted to women on welfare. A jealous abuser will find it easier to suppress a woman on welfare who has nothing and lacks the skills or economic ability to stand up for herself. The young welfare recipient will be more intrinsically dependent on her intimate partner from the beginning—the "perfect mate" for an abuser who doesn't

want his partner out in the wider world. Because of their low educational levels and occupational status, abusers who are poor know they
can't search for a mate from the pool of those women who are successful in the world of employment.

Bernice says that welfare recipients, isolated from the world of
work, stay in their own tightly locked communities. She believes that
girls and women on welfare thus are magnets for men who are abusers.
Not only are women on welfare not out in the wider world, an environment so threatening to the abuser, but (in the past at least) they also
generally have had no motivation to join that world. In other words,
explains Bernice, they aren't going anywhere.

> As a welfare recipient, I knew that society didn't accept me. I was
> in a different total class. An untouchable class. Women on welfare
> know that they are an untouchable class, that is how they are seen.
> Because they are already suppressed by being on welfare, these women
> are already there. All the abusers have to do is to maintain the
> situation. We have nothing, and we don't know how to stand up for
> ourselves. That is why abusers encourage welfare usage. With wel-
> fare, you are being given something, but that something really stig-
> matizes you out in society. That stigma lowers your self-esteem and
> keeps you in line.

⚜

"When it pays not to work" is the heading of a recent letter to the
editor of a newspaper from a woman who left welfare for work and
found herself less well off economically than before. "Explain to me
and my children how we are better off with my having a job," she
writes.[18] Although it is important that women like these who work not
be worse off than if they remain on welfare, women need to understand
the other important, nonfinancial benefits that accrue to them and their
households through productive work. Bernice's experiences force us to
explore the value of work in general for women's self-esteem and ability to stay free of violence.

Having a partner dependent on him financially increases a man's
own sense of masculinity and personal power. Power relationships
within the family may change if the male's partner has her own source
of funds. The huge emphasis that abusers put on employment of their

partners indicates the importance of work for battered women. Indeed, most studies have found that women's employment modifies the gender division of labor within the household and may also imply changes in the balance of power between men and women within the family.[19] Studies of women within developing countries find that, as women become employed outside the home, they gain greater freedom and control within the family.[20] It appears that abusers' hunches about the effects of employment for their partners are right on the mark.

In addition to providing the capacity for much-needed economic independence, however, work provides other necessary ingredients that help women escape from and stay free of violence. These critical attributes of employment include instilling a sense of personal worth and value, a sense of purpose and achievement, a capacity to contribute to the wider society, experience with and control over social arrangements outside the household, and independence from the control of others.[21]

Bernice's story demonstrates the importance of work for human development. During her first few years at work, she believes, she learned on the job most of the skills she needed in building a new life for herself and her children. "That job was my mother. The workplace was my learning tool." The process went like this: First of all, Bernice says, she became competent in her ability to perform her job duties. After about four or five months her clients started letting her know that she was doing well. As a result Bernice was motivated to try to conquer her insomnia because she wanted to perform well the next day. The students gave her a sense of normality; they made Bernice want to eat right, sleep right, be energetic, look positive, and stay strong.

> It made me feel so good. It opened up a whole new life for me. I had never had anything in my life that I felt I was good at. To have positive input from not just two to three people, but from a whole group, that I wasn't ugly or dumb, that I was smart, that I had something I could give to people, there was some goodness in me. I always wanted to be productive, I wanted people to see that I could be dedicated and they could be appreciative just for having me around. When a student would say, "Bernice, I am so glad that you came to work today," it would make me feel wonderful. When a student would say, "I need to come talk to you," that was heaven.

For Bernice, the workplace represented the outside validation that she was a person of worth and value. Success at work jump-started her recovery process.

> This was serious. This wasn't a therapist cheerleading me on. You had to believe it yourself. This was breathtaking for me. I was creating a whole new identity.

Could Bernice have created the new identity as an effective person without work? She doesn't think so.

> Work is tied to my self-esteem. My job gives me worth, it allows me to know that I am valuable. That I am paid because I have skills. I can make things happen. I can help other women. Every client that I help, I have power.

For Bernice, work is also an important part of not being a domestic violence victim.

> Work to me is almost like life and death. It is everything. I would be afraid that I wouldn't have an identity, that I would slip back into a person that didn't want anything, that life would not have any value. Every day that I come to work, I'm one day ahead of not being in a domestic violence relationship, not being homeless. I go to school, I don't use drugs, I don't drink, I don't gamble. I don't ever want to be in a situation where I feel powerless. Being an employee means standing on your own two feet, it means power over fear.

In addition to the strength and affirmation that employment gives her, it is also important that work is not welfare.

> Society doesn't accept women on welfare. We working women represent today's society. Society accepts me now. That is a big part of my self-esteem. I don't want anyone to support me. I don't want any systems to support me. I have the strength in my own body to get out and do and to learn.
>
> To me, being off welfare means that I know how to work. It means that I know how to be committed and dedicated. It stands for

a lot of different things in my life. A symbol of everything. I am free. I am competent. The world has some value for me. I can have dreams. Nobody is in control of my life. I have power over me. That is all I ever wanted is power over me. I never wanted anything else. I don't care what I have to do, I don't ever want to have to go back to welfare. It would be like sticking a knife in my heart. Being off welfare means being alive.

As we have seen, the therapeutic process for sexual assault and physical violence involves the need to reconnect to and find one's proper place in the wider world. The outside validation of self-worth that work provides on so many levels, from a sense of efficacy on the job to acceptance by society, is an important therapeutic ingredient for low-income battered women like Bernice who have never worked.

Next, Bernice describes how the skills she learned on the job helped her outside the workplace. At work Bernice discovered that she had a certain responsibility, that her supervisor had certain duties, and that the executive director had other tasks. She learned on the job to say, this is what I can do. She observed workers coming together to solve a problem or reach a common goal, with each bringing something to the table. She saw workers arguing their points, sticking up for their viewpoints, and watched as consensus emerged. This was a process she had never seen in action before in her life.

Working taught Bernice how to make decisions, wise decisions. At work she learned new things, met new people, and overcame obstacles on a daily basis. But most importantly, Bernice says, her work allowed her to know that if she did make a mistake, it could be rectified the next day. "I learned to keep doing it until I got it right. Don't destroy yourself because you did something wrong."

As the days went by, Bernice carried these work learnings over to other aspects of her life. For example, she says she was scared to talk with Little Billy's teacher who told Bernice that her son didn't know his ABCs. Bernice knew that Billy could recite the alphabet; she had heard him doing it at home. Yet the teacher was always lecturing her about Bernice's dysfunctional family and laying the blame there. Bernice said she was always too scared to tell the teacher that her son did know the material. Now she tells Jessica's teacher, "This is what I am willing to do. What are you willing to do to meet me halfway?" Bernice says she

is now able to hold the teacher responsible for what the school is supposed to be doing.

Bernice found out she was eligible for transitional medical assistance after she began work, but she was turned down by her welfare
caseworker.

> I said, "Yes, I am eligible," and then I looked at the caseworker and
> said, "Where do you go to file an appeal?" He nearly fell out of that
> chair. And I filed an appeal and I won. And I also changed the terms
> under which the worker and I interacted. I protested his practice of
> making me come to the office every month to get the medical card,
> and obtained a card good for six months. I became competent in my
> abilities to advocate for my family and myself. I became an effective
> person for the first time in my life.

What Bernice learned on the job enabled her to put it all together.

> When you are on public aid, you are in a state of total submission.
> You are dominated by the caseworkers. Your child's teachers put you
> down. This is all a form of suppression, to keep you quiet, not to
> have a life, not to have an opinion.

As Bernice's supervisor helped her sort through personality conflicts at
the workplace, Bernice realized that she had the right not to be abused
by co-workers on the job. This learning she then transferred to her
relationship with her own mother. When her mother called on the
telephone and was abusive to her, Bernice says, she learned to terminate
the conversation.

Karen Brown, formerly with the City Works (Bronx, New York)
welfare-to-work program, describes the transformations that working
causes for welfare recipients. "I do observe that our students take more
pride in their paychecks than their AFDC check," she wrote me in a
letter. "Often they have well-thought-out plans for what they will do
with it (i.e., help their mother out, buy much-needed clothes for their
children, save towards a better apartment, etc.)." She continued:

> I think there is much more ownership of one's paycheck
> because one worked for it than the AFDC check, which

comes automatically for nothing. Also, being out in the world at work raises the overall expectation of our program graduates—they see what they don't have and start making careful plans to improve their lives and the lives of their children (i.e., doing well on the job, starting community college, etc.) This is qualitatively different from AFDC receipt and this may create friction with the boyfriend/father of the child. [22]

Social scientists agree with Bernice about the role of productive work in human development. Self-esteem is a concept tied to one's basic identity. And work builds basic identity because it is involvement outside oneself.[23] According to Katherine Newman, who has extensively interviewed low-income workers in Harlem, exclusion from the society of the employed is "a devastating source of social isolation. We could hand people money, as various guaranteed-income plans of the past thirty years have suggested. But we can't hand out honor. Honor comes from participation in this central setting in our culture and from the positive identity it confers."[24]

It is also important to remember that poverty is a multidimensional phenomenon and does not signify merely a relative lack of income. To escape poverty permanently, the poor must take part in the provision of their own needs rather than relying on the state to solve their problems, and to do so they must first acquire the means to become more self-sufficient. One analyst has identified eight bases of social power, the principal means available to a household to become and remain self-reliant. These are listed here to demonstrate the requirements and linkages that poor women must make and maintain to stay free from poverty.

1. Defensible space
2. Surplus time
3. Knowledge and skills and investment of time, energy, and money in the development of the household's human resources
4. Access to appropriate information
5. Access to social organizations that connect the household with the outer society

6. Social networks (family, neighbors, friends)
7. Health
8. Financial resources[25]

When looked at in this broader way it becomes clear that poor families will remove themselves from poverty only by a developmental process that involves a commitment to the development of the skills and talents of household members and a linkage of the family to information, support, and assistance from institutions and social networks in the wider world.

It is this wider linkage that the abuser works diligently to destroy. Battered women report that they are not allowed to establish friendships, visit family members, upgrade their basic skills, or participate in activities offered by institutions in the community. Little Billy, for example, was not permitted to attend summer camp. Jessica could not be left at a child care center. Bernice could not have a friend visit, telephone friends, or even go to the grocery store unattended.

The philosopher Martha Nussbaum posits ten central human functional capabilities, arguing that politics should focus on moving as many people as possible into a state of capacity to function with respect to this interlocking set of capabilities. Nussbaum's conceptual framework is useful as we consider the role played by domestic violence in creating women's poverty. These central human capacities include being able to imagine, to think, and to reason; having the capacity to engage in critical reflection about the planning of one's own life; possessing the social bases of self-respect and nonhumiliation; and being able to be treated as a dignified being whose worth is equal to that of others—all capabilities expressed over and over again by Bernice as the essence of her own self-esteem. Continues Nussbaum:

> When the capabilities are deprived of the nourishment that
> would transform them into the high-level capabilities that
> figure on my list, they are fruitless, cut off, in some way but
> a shadow of themselves. They are like actors who never get
> to go on the stage, or a person who sleeps all through life,
> or a musical score that is never performed.[26]

Not only does domestic violence keep many low-income women out of the labor market, but it also prevents them from developing the

120   wherewithal to create the essential sense of self—or the central human capabilities—that make such activity even remotely possible. As one commentator has remarked, "Poverty is not deprivation. It is isolation."[27] So domestic violence is more serious than other welfare-to-work barriers—serious because of how it closes off knowledge, connections, and opportunities for women that give them the power to improve their own circumstances. This is the very essence of how domestic violence traps women and keeps them in poverty.

For battered women, work thus represents a critical means of empowerment. But how can our welfare policies encourage work for battered women while at the same time keep them safe from harm?

CHAPTER EIGHT

Toward New Public Policy

All activity of the mind should be so encouraged that there will always be in existence a nucleus of women who think, invent, imagine, and create as freely as men do, and with little fear of ridicule and condescension. . . . if such opinions [to the contrary] prevail in the future we shall remain in a condition of half-civilised barbarism. At least that is how I define an eternity of domination on the one hand and of servility on the other. For the degradation of being a slave is only equalled by the degradation of being a master.

—VIRGINIA WOOLF, *"The Intellectual Status of Women"*

In a recent memoir, the writer Rosemary Bray recounts her life in a family on welfare in Chicago. Bray's father was an abuser who frequently beat his wife and children severely. Bray writes that compliance with the provisions of the 1996 Federal welfare reform law would have resulted in more domestic violence for her mother and the children.

There would have been no one to be with us after school, no one to intervene between me and my father's endless rages. And my mother's absence from home would have fueled my father's persistent jealousy. A man who could not tolerate his wife's grocery shopping would have been hard-pressed to accept her going to school eight hours a day with strangers. No, this plan for self-sufficiency would have meant the disintegration of my already fragile family life.

Had it been in place thirty years earlier, the new welfare bill would have taken my mother out of our home each day. Mama would have been required to attend a training program, in the hope that two years of training to work in food services or day care would serve as an adequate educational supplement to the third-grade education she had gotten a generation earlier. The four of us children, on the other hand, would have been left to fend for ourselves after school, in one of the worse neighborhoods of the United States.[1]

Like Bernice and Rosemary Bray's mother a generation ago, many women on welfare who are current victims of domestic violence may be unable to meet their state's work-related requirements without subjecting themselves and their children to serious danger of one kind or another.

In May 1998 the *Washington Post* reported a welfare-to-work story that had gone seriously wrong. Antoinette Goode, twenty-nine years of age, had completed a training course from which she emerged as the natural leader of the thirteen participating welfare recipients. Classmates reported that the stalking of her ex-boyfriend got worse and worse during the training. They observed him following Goode at lunch hour. After completing her training course Goode landed a job in 1997 with the federal Office of Personnel Management and subsequently won a promotion.

But Goode still had trouble with her children's father. At the end of May 1997 she was told that her ex-boyfriend was making threats against her. Frightened, she sought a new order of protection, which was denied because the threats were, according to the court intake worker, secondhand in nature. Antoinette Goode, a welfare-to-work success story, became a fatality statistic the next day. As her son and daughter watched in terror, she was stabbed to death as she walked home from a bus stop in Alexandria, Virginia.[2]

Will abusers let women go to work knowing that if they do not, welfare benefits will be lost? In sixty-minute interviews with twenty-four respondents in her neighborhood study, Susan Lloyd found that some women decrease their work or fail to work because of partner interference, while others increase their work effort to reduce their reliance on husbands or boyfriends for economic security:

> The in-depth accounts point to differences in the individual characteristics and life circumstances of the women. For example, as noted elsewhere, paid employment enabled some women to respond to male violence by ending abusive relationships. In other instances, women's exits from harmful circumstances were conditioned on their access to different kinds of resources and on their status as mothers as well as providers. The majority of the women who participated in long interviews stressed the need for access to and personal control over money and other resources in order to be able to leave an abusive partner.[3]

Anecdotal evidence from around the country suggests several different scenarios. Even when they are allowed to attend mandatory education, training, workfare programs, or employment, some women report that they receive harsh physical punishment at home. This kind of suffering is unconscionable. Better policy would have welfare departments assess domestic violence and provide services to help eliminate the abuse before women undertake labor market responsibilities. There are other instances in which, even though women are required to participate in work, their partners actively sabotage their activities or harass them on the job, eventually preventing their employment. Absent information, counseling, and support, many of these women cannot work out a way to extricate themselves into safety, and they may remain in the relationship but off welfare as a result. Still other battered women may never have thought about work and cannot even envision themselves out of the house in the wider world. For these women, the combination of violence and poverty also traps them in a situation that will certainly result in their remaining with their abuser and ultimately off welfare.

Even within the straitjacket of the time requirements of the new Temporary Assistance to Needy Families program (TANF), it is possible for welfare departments to sort out these cases and to attempt to provide needed help and resources. In response to the issue of domestic violence, welfare departments should be encouraged to provide as much

individualized assistance as possible to help battered women make a
safe transition to work.

As welfare reform was initially being considered by the U.S. Senate
in 1996, Senators Paul Wellstone (D, Minnesota) and Patty Murray (D,
Washington) successfully amended the bill with a provision now
known as the Family Violence Option.[4] Under the Family Violence Option, if a state choosing to implement the option assesses domestic violence and refers a battered woman on welfare to domestic violence
services, it may temporarily waive the twenty-four-month work requirement and the sixty-month lifetime limit on receipt of federal benefits, among others, and can escape federal financial penalties for failure
to have the requisite number of women working each month. Although
assessment of domestic violence within welfare offices is difficult at best
and surely will result in many women choosing not to divulge their
circumstances, the Family Violence Option gives battered women the
chance to obtain needed help for the domestic violence before they
tackle work issues. With the motto of "safety first" welfare departments
can craft policies and procedures that can go a long way toward helping
battered women rather than harming them.

Although, as we have seen, many abusers control where their partner can go, most battered women say they are allowed to visit the
welfare department office, even though the abuser may insist on driving
them there and may sit in the waiting room or wait for them in the
parking lot. Since most welfare departments do not allow the partners
to accompany the women when they are called for their interview,
the appointment provides a critical opportunity to provide information
about domestic violence to these extremely isolated women.

Recently one westside Chicago welfare office played a large role in
one recipient's escape from domestic violence into safety. Upon request
of the client's domestic violence advocate, the welfare case manager
sent a letter to the victim, mandating an appointment and ordering the
woman to bring her children along. As usual, her partner drove her
to the welfare office. When she and the children were called in, by
prearrangement a police car was ready in the back alley to transport
them to a suburban domestic violence shelter. Eventually the woman
settled permanently in this new community, found full-time employment, and now is off the welfare rolls.[5]

In addition to meeting safety concerns, the Family Violence Option enables welfare departments to bring specialized domestic violence services to women on welfare, giving many of these women the opportunity to go through a recovery process for the first time, even as they may be attempting to engage in work activities. We have seen that many victims and survivors need to deal with a number of issues, including flashbacks, anger, or depression, with which a formal recovery process can greatly assist. Thus, one of the goals of welfare policy is to provide low-income girls and women the opportunity to recover fully from the trauma in a way that promotes their empowerment and gives them enough information so they can cope with the effects of the violence over the rest of their lives. Most low-income women struggle with these issues on their own, in isolation. Welfare reform is also the opportunity to bring needed interventions for children who have been traumatized by viewing the violence.

Other activities can be especially useful for battered women, including literacy training that rebuilds low basic skills and concomitant low social esteem, vocational exploration, and "work hardening," which consists of allowing a domestic violence victim to spend limited time in a work setting, with the time gradually increasing. Performing limited work activities allows the survivor to experience and develop her competency in a work setting or public arena.[6]

Early information about implementation of the Family Violence Option provides no real grounds for optimism about possible welfare department intervention. Although most states have chosen to implement the provisions of the Family Violence Option, as of the spring of 1999 few women appeared to be disclosing the domestic violence in their lives to their welfare workers. There is considerable doubt whether welfare case workers are actually telling women about the option, and it is unclear whether the women understand that they can so disclose without penalties and with full confidentiality. It is likely that many battered women simply will not entrust the disclosure of their abuse to a government worker.

For this reason, some welfare departments have, in some locations, hired or colocated trained domestic violence advocates in department offices who perform education and screening of domestic violence. Preliminary data indicate that women feel more comfortable confiding in a nongovernmental employee, and welfare workers also are relieved that they do not have to delve into personal matters with their clients.[7]

126   However, the expense connected with these schemes has generally prohibited their widespread expansion, although they hold out much hope
of success.

Bernice herself strongly urges that welfare workers inquire about
domestic violence, and ask about it often. Welfare case workers should
also be trained to pick up on and respond to cues from their clients.
Although Bernice says that she would often weep in front of her case
worker, she was never asked why she was crying. Today Bernice is
certain that if she had been queried she would have seized the opportunity to confess the situation. Bernice emphasizes how important it
would have been for her to have received some basic information about
domestic violence resources. For example, she never knew there was
such a thing as a domestic violence shelter.

> It is so important for the welfare department to work with young
> girls. It would have been hard to work with me being resistant, or
> being embarrassed or ashamed, but I so needed to be in a position
> where I was getting some kind of education. I had tried to leave a
> few times. If I had understood about domestic violence, I would have
> tried harder when I left. I didn't know how to stay gone. I didn't
> know they get more violent when you try to leave. I needed help with
> a safety plan. I needed shelter, because I had nowhere to go. If I had
> had someone tell me about teens and violence, the fact that you can
> restart your life, I would have taken it. I was getting no input from
> the outside world, the real world, the world that functions. All my
> input was coming from dysfunctional points. The welfare department
> just has to make it easier for us to tell them what is going on.

In Bernice's case, for starters, the welfare department could have simply
tried not to make matters worse. Only recently did I find out that after
Bernice was dismissed from her licensed practical nursing program she
was sanctioned—cut off welfare—because she was back at home not
engaged in a work-related or training activity. Although she then told
her worker the cause of her dismissal, no domestic violence service
referrals were ever offered.

Then there was the matter of the babysitting checks. Bernice asked
her worker to send her child care checks to another address, because
each time the check came home, Billy got to it first and tore it up.

Naturally, Bernice's babysitter was irate because she hadn't been paid. Until Bernice established new living arrangements for herself and the children, the department said it had to continue to send the checks to her home, unless Bernice could establish a post office box, which she couldn't afford. Bernice remembers one time that she had to go to Billy's after she had just moved in with her mother to retrieve the check before Billy could get to it. She wasn't successful. Billy beat Bernice badly that day and tore up the check again.

And when Bernice got her first job, her case worker made an error and cut her case completely off, despite Bernice's eligibility for transitional medical assistance and food stamps. Ultimately she filed an appeal and obtained the benefits to which she was entitled a year later.

Federal welfare reform now gives the states the flexibility to devise innovative approaches that could greatly assist battered women on welfare who may need onetime assistance with security deposits or the first month's rent, money for the purchase of a car to increase safety, or other more long-term assistance with transitional housing needs. Oregon's policy can serve as a model. Although there is a $350 maximum for any emergency, battered women can qualify for up to $1,200 with no payback by the participant. Funds can be used for housing and utility costs or relocation, for example. In November 1997, the state reports, it spent approximately $128,000 for emergency assistance for domestic violence victims for housing and utility costs, and $153,000 in December 1997.[8] Many battered women need a small amount of financial assistance to relocate successfully. With a few exceptions, no state has really taken a good look at using welfare emergency assistance funds to facilitate and support women's escape plans.

It is also important to remember that for some women who have escaped the violence, getting on welfare may be a very good thing; without welfare benefits women are unable to leave a domestic violence shelter and establish a new home. As we have seen, because many women continue to suffer from problems after they leave their abuser, including stalking, child custody battles, and severe physical and mental health problems, the victims may well need welfare for a period of time to stabilize their lives. The current political emphasis on welfare-to-work often obscures the role that welfare should and must play for battered women who are in the process of escaping their situation. To ensure that this safety net exists, welfare departments must be sensitive and flexible enough to take the needs of battered women into account. Welfare offices, for example, that direct all new applicants into job search or work search activities, even before approving their grant applications, are in danger of causing more damage to some battered women and their children. Some battered women will be able to start a job immediately, others may need a much longer period of healing, and still others may never be able to enter the workforce. Devising these individual plans is difficult in the current welfare reform environment that monolithically pushes applicants and recipients into jobs, but it can be done if there is the political will.

✤

When women leave their abusers we have seen that the violence and abuse often escalate and become more deadly. Women who leave welfare and go to work often face harassment at the workplace, often resulting in job loss. What can be done to assist women in these situations? One anecdote will suffice to illustrate the major problem. Because her ex-partner continually called her at work, using fake voices to get through, a Maine woman was forced to resign from her job. Her employer was unwilling to risk an incident of violence due to a previous unrelated domestic violence incident at her workplace. "There was a woman who was going through a divorce and whose husband was always coming into her workplace. She was told to get a restraining order or she would be suspended. He later killed her and himself."[9] All too often, employers, traumatized and made afraid by a previous violent incident at the workplace, try to prevent further incidents by firing or forcing victims of domestic violence to resign. This approach, of course, colludes with abusers and encourages their workplace harassment. Battered women's shelters have the same security fears as employers. Some shelters actually require women to quit their jobs once they enter a shelter, so that the abuser cannot follow them from work to the shelter.

Although battered women do need safe and reliable child care, and could benefit from case management services to help them deal with domestic violence issues after they reach the workplace, what they really need are employers in whom they can confide about domestic violence, and who can work with the women to minimize its effects at the workplace. Employers could, for example, temporarily transfer employees to work stations where they might be freer from harassment (like a move from the front desk) or might assist with more security at the workplace.

Bernice introduced me to Corrina, a welfare recipient who is now employed part-time at a welfare-to-work program. Corinna, who lives in one of the most dangerous high-rise public housing apartment complexes, had to evict her abuser from her home before she was able to go to work. When I met Corinna she was just back to work after a one-month stay in a battered women's shelter. At the first of last month her ex-partner, a drug addict, came to her apartment, severely beat her, and took the money from her newly cashed paycheck, including the funds for the rent due the next day. Corinna went to a domestic violence shelter, but because all the city's shelter beds were full, she was taken to a refuge in the western suburbs, inaccessible to work by public transportation. It took two weeks for a bed to open up in a nearby shelter. Luckily Corinna's employer held her job open for her. Would all employers have been as generous?

It remains highly unlikely, however, that welfare departments will be motivated to work with and educate employers in this regard. With the federally mandated work requirements and concomitant financial penalties for states who fail to meet them, there is every incentive for welfare departments to minimize the social and skill barriers presented by welfare recipients so as to help them make the transition to the workplace as soon as possible. In one southeastern state, the welfare department did not want any information about the prevalence of domestic violence in its caseloads released to me, lest, after the ensuing publicity, employers refuse to hire welfare recipients in their state.[10]

These are not easy issues. Recently Pat Prinzevalle, director of a battered women's shelter in the St. Paul, Minnesota area, told me that when she had recent staff vacancies she hired four welfare recipients because she believed she should do her part in welfare reform. Of the four, two turned out to be battered women. One battered employee's former partner recently kidnapped her child, and the other employee is currently being stalked. In both circumstances the employees are not able to perform their duties at the shelter owing to the domestic violence in their own lives.

As a survivor of domestic violence herself, Prinzevalle is extremely apologetic about raising the issue. An employer, she says, must be sensitive and supportive about the issue of domestic violence. Yet the work must get done—ironically, in this instance, the important job of helping battered women in crisis. How many accommodations should an employer be required to make?[11]

And now comes the moment when I must detail my own recent experience with hiring a victim of domestic violence on my own staff. In the winter of 1998 I recruited Anita from another agency, where she had worked for five years as an administrative assistant. Anita had made it her business to let me know that she had finally escaped a violent marriage five years ago and had been a victim of serious stalking for some time after that.

Things were going pretty well until Anita was involved in an automobile accident in the spring of 1998 that totally destroyed her car and left her badly injured. When she returned to work about a month later, Anita was a shadow of her former self. Unfocused, she had difficulty completing even simple tasks without error. Her telephone messages were garbled and her usual good judgment had deserted her. Anita's panic was mirrored in her eyes.

When I eventually discussed her job performance, Anita confided that the accident was causing her to have flashbacks to her years of domestic violence, which were causing sleeplessness and terror. After speaking with Anita, the counselor in our Employee Assistance Program told her he thought she was suffering from posttraumatic stress disorder and needed immediate treatment. Many weeks passed and Anita did not seek professional help. Ultimately, I had to terminate her employment with a generous severance package because Anita was unable to perform any aspect of her job.

All of the knowledge we have gained about domestic violence mandates that as a society we intervene earlier than we do. We have seen how many young girls become sexually active and form partnerships as a result of sexual assault and abuse in their own childhoods. Emerging data suggest that violence is more prevalent in teen relationships than in those involving older women.

According to the National Crime Victimization Survey, the highest rates of violence affect girls and women ages sixteen through twenty-four, about 20 women per 1,000, as compared to rates of 16.5 per

1,000 for women ages twenty-five through thirty-four, and 7 per 1,000 for women thirty-five through forty-nine years of age.[12]

A disproportionate number of reported rape victims are teen girls. In 1992, for example, 62 percent of all forcible rape cases involved victims who were younger than seventeen years of age; 32 percent of victims of rape were between eleven and seventeen years old, and 29 percent of victims were younger than eleven years old. In 1996 convicted rape and sexual assault offenders serving time in state prisons reported that two-thirds of their victims were under the age of eighteen, and 58 percent reported that their victims were twelve and younger.[13]

A study of domestic violence victimization conducted in Chicago Department of Public Health clinics corroborates this overrepresentation of abuse within populations of younger women. Younger victims outnumbered older women by two to one: although 31 percent of females seventeen and under were violence victims within the last year, and 28 percent between eighteen and nineteen, and 20.6 percent between twenty and twenty-four, only 15.4 percent between twenty-five and twenty-nine were victims. Only 13 percent of those forty and over were domestic violence victims.[14]

The few studies looking at domestic violence among adolescents have found that teens suffered significantly higher rates of abuse during pregnancy than adult women. Twenty-six percent of pregnant teens in a West Virginia study had been abused, compared with 10 percent of adult women. In two other research studies, teens reported 22 percent, as compared to 16 percent of adults, and 33 percent of teens as compared with less than one-quarter of adult women who were battered during pregnancy.[15] The Chicago Department of Health also found that 21 percent of the domestic violence victims had suffered abuse during pregnancy, and the majority of the abuse was physical.[16]

Teen girls are also subject to sexual assault at alarming rates. National data released in 1997 indicate that for 21 percent of females ages fifteen through nineteen who first had sex at age fourteen or younger, their first experience was not voluntary, compared to 12 percent whose first sex occurred at age sixteen, and 7 percent whose first sexual experience occurred at age nineteen. In general, the data indicate that the younger a girl is when she first has sex, the more likely it is that first sexual experience is nonvoluntary.[17]

The Commonwealth Fund Survey of the Health of Adolescent Girls, a study conducted by Louis Harris and Associates, gave questionnaires to 6,748 adolescents in 265 public, private, and parochial schools in grades five through twelve. That research found that one in four girls in grades nine through twelve said she had been physically and sexually abused or had experienced forced sex with a boyfriend, disturbingly high rates of abuse. Of those who said they had been abused, 53 percent said the abuse took place in their homes, 65 percent stated it had happened more than once, 57 percent said they had been abused by a family member, and 13 percent reported the abuser was a family friend. Half of the girls who stated they had been sexually abused said they had also experienced physical abuse. Eight percent of high school girls said they had been forced by a boyfriend or a date to have sex against their will.[18]

A recent study on dating violence surveyed 635 students between the ages of thirteen and eighteen from a large midwestern high school containing a good representative sampling of African Americans, Asians, and Hispanics. Almost 18 percent of the girls stated they had been subjected to forced sexual activity; 22.5 percent reported severe physical violence. Respondents also reported their perceptions about why the violence or abuse occurred. Boys reporting they had been subject to a partner's use of physical violence (17 percent) stated that the reason for the violence was their making sexual advances toward their dating partner. Only 3 percent of the girls reported they were subject to violence as a result of their own sexual advances toward their partner. Moreover, the girls reported they were victims of physical violence significantly more often while their male boyfriends were making sexual advances. Thirty-seven percent of the girls stated they were subjected to physical violence because their partner had been making sexual advances toward them. "This suggests that a large percentage of girls are being abused because they are refusing unwanted sexual advances." The researchers conclude that many males begin abusive behavior toward female partners early in the life cycle, and attempts to identify and intervene with violent boys as early as possible seem warranted.[19]

Another recent dating violence study involving 1,012 students enrolled in public high schools in the Los Angeles area also found 17 percent of the females reporting forced sexual acts. Forty-five and a half percent of the females and 43 percent of males reported they had received some form of physical aggression from dating partners at least once during the course of dating. Among female victims, the most frequently chosen reason for the partners' use of violence was jealousy, corresponding to common patterns in adult domestic violence situations. Interestingly, on several individual violence items (e.g., being slapped and hit with a fist or object), males reported more dating violence than females. For the sexual force item, females reported significantly more violence than males. The researchers concluded that it is likely that some of the violence that males received resulted from forcing sexual activities on their partners.[20] Both dating violence studies underscore the need for early intervention to reduce violence in teen relationships.

Although information about the shockingly high prevalence of domestic violence among teenagers has emerged, researchers and evaluators of teen welfare-to-work efforts have to date failed to integrate this knowledge into research designs. For example, an evaluation of three different demonstration projects for teen parents on welfare found that the teen mothers who had already dropped out of school when they entered the program had barely responded to the program's financial incentives. Both their earnings and school completion rates were essentially the same as the control group. The evaluators commented that many teens simply cannot conform to the orderly schedule of economic independence that the government would like to impose on them. The newspaper report on the evaluation stated that the group "is too damaged mentally or physically even for the most desperate employer."[21] But consider an alternate approach: if we had a way to assess for the prevalence of current domestic violence in these girls' lives, might we not find that these interventions work well for those teens who are not involved with abusive or controlling boyfriends, but work poorly for those who are?

In this regard, data from one of the few published studies on teens, education, and partner behavior is extremely provocative. In a multisite longitudinal evaluation of teen pregnancy and parenting project demonstration programs, researchers found that living with a boyfriend or husband had a significant correlation with the teens dropping out of school (19 percent of the sample was living with a partner). Project coordinators believed that jealousy played a role; male partners may

134   encourage the girls to be truant so they will not meet other boys in school. One program that involved the male partner as well as his girl-friend was more successful in increasing school attendance. Similar re-sults were found in a follow-up study of sixty-five Hispanic and African American teen mothers in Arizona, where boyfriend support was the most significant predictor of school status. The researchers commented, "Specifically, the dynamics of the relationship between teenagers and their partners and the mechanism by which partner support and school drop-out are related must be discerned, so that interventions can be devised which help teen mothers complete school."[22] In other words, instead of studying the characteristics of the teen girls, it would be more productive to focus on the behavior of their male partners.

Teenagers are a particularly important group to target as their vio-lent childhood experiences begin to overlap with their intimate rela-tionships as burgeoning adults. Bernice's story well illustrates the price we pay when we ignore the fact that "it is the relationship, stupid." Would early and effective intervention with teens on welfare around violence issues have saved Bernice thirteen years of violence that inter-fered with her critical personal development? Bernice thinks that in her extreme isolation she would have grabbed every scrap of information provided about relationships and domestic violence. One thing is cer-tain: Bernice's story, and what data we have about horrific levels of violence in the lives of teen girls, require us to refocus and dedicate resources to low-income girls—the intervention that can have the big-gest payoff.

※

What would early intervention look like? Even though we have seen that violence and sexual assault are critical issues for low-income com-munities, in most of our low-income neighborhoods no services are organized around the issue of violence for either children or adults. In the main, girls and women must deal with these issues on their own and in isolation, effectively barring them from obtaining the support and therapy they need to escape from and recover from these experi-ences.

To make matters even worse, many social service agencies have not yet perceived that interpersonal violence may be the underlying cause of the problems that their clients are manifesting. Parenting classes, for example, address only a symptom of the underlying problem of violence; if the mother is being beaten on a daily basis, certainly her parenting skills—indeed, her ability to relate to the outside world—will suffer. Children viewing the violence will act out in serious ways that put additional pressure on parenting skills. Techniques learned in a parenting class cannot entirely deal with the issue. Although every parent can benefit from parenting classes, services delivered in isolation from other major issues are bound to fail. One program director gave me an example. She told of a seventeen-year old immigrant girl, a victim of severe abuse from her intimate partner, who is the father of her child. The child is now under the jurisdiction of the state child protection agency, which has mandated that the young woman attend a parenting group. But her abuser will not let her attend the group and continually sets up roadblocks. Unless the young woman discloses the live-in presence of the abuser in her life, she is in danger of losing custody of her child. Yet she is terrified of the backlash from her partner.[23]

Nor are most health providers and mental health professionals well versed in the issue of interpersonal violence. The Better Homes Fund comments, "Training to increase health clinicians' awareness of the prevalence and indicators of abuse and assault and the link with physical and mental health sequelae is a crucial beginning. Education about interpersonal violence should be integrated into undergraduate and graduate level curricula as well as continuing education programs for clinicians."[24]

There are a minimum of seven basic elements that would constitute a communitywide response to domestic violence:

- All helping professionals need in-depth training in interpersonal violence and its assessment. Every social service agency should have a protocol in place to screen girls and women for domestic violence as well as its effects.
- Each community should establish a rape crisis center that has the capacity to provide immediate responses to women and girls who have been victims of sexual assault.
- Every low-income community must have the capacity of providing more formal mental health counseling for those with more extreme effects of trauma such as posttraumatic stress disorder and substance abuse.

• Providers should secure access to relevant services by creating referral networks and an awareness of necessary services outside the community of which residents can avail themselves.

• Each community should develop a series of self-help groups that can provide needed support in the areas of domestic violence, incest survivors group, Alcoholics Anonymous, rape survivors, and the like. Former victims who serve as volunteers to assist others similarly situated should lead these groups.

• All teachers, school personnel, and child care workers should be trained to assess for interpersonal violence or child sexual molestation when they observe a child in their care with behavioral problems to make certain that children suffering sexual assault in childhood and current victims of domestic violence receive prompt therapeutic intervention.

• Each community should establish a broad-based and inclusive system that can provide information to every girl and woman about sexual assault and domestic violence as well as community resources available to her.

In a 1997 study of domestic violence in the London borough of Hackney, researchers surveyed the files of key social service agencies in the area to ascertain the number of cases relating to domestic violence. Although the study's own survey of women in physician waiting rooms found high levels of current domestic violence, agency records revealed far fewer women availing themselves of assistance for domestic violence. Despite their admitting that interpersonal violence was a major problem in this low-income area of London, few agencies had incorporated monitoring or assessment of domestic violence as a "part of everyday practice." The researchers concluded that given the high prevalence of domestic violence in the community, the importance of asking women directly about domestic violence cannot be overstated.[25]

As vital as it is to ensure that basic support services are available in all of our communities for girls and women violence victims, we must also be more creative in envisioning new responses. Carol Goertzel, director of the Women's Association for Women's Alternatives in Montgomery County, Pennsylvania, believes that hotlines are one important answer for women violence victims. Although they are not able to leave the house to attend support groups or even parenting classes, those with telephones might be able to talk with someone on a regular basis for information and support. Telephone hotlines could be an important lifeline for some low-income girls and women.[26]

Placing domestic violence counseling within welfare department offices themselves would also greatly improve women's access to these services. On many occasions Bernice has suggested that the welfare office is the safest and best location for family planning services for low-income girls and women who are unable to visit health clinics on their own. Every teen parent on welfare should also be required to attend at least one special workshop about domestic violence, optimally taught by an experienced domestic violence provider at the welfare department office.

Innovation and creativity should be fostered and rewarded. Such efforts to reach out to girls and women need not be expensive. One woman in Hackney was able to leave her violent partner simply because she discovered the telephone number of Women's Aid printed on the back of her rent bill.[27] How can battered women on welfare, who are by definition isolated, find out where to get help? Unfortunately, we have discovered the issue of domestic violence at a time when many welfare departments have ceased sending written material to welfare homes. For example, departments are implementing direct deposit of welfare checks and debit cards for such benefits as food stamps. However, every mailing from a welfare department can and should include information that can assist battered women to reach out. Utility bills could also be a useful place for the provision of basic information.

Historically, battered women's shelters have been overwhelmed with their own tasks at hand and have had to respond to a large need with inadequate resources. For this reason many have been simply unable to serve as the catalyst for creating such a network of services in their communities. The fact that the shelters are in hidden locations within their neighborhoods, although necessary to ensure the safety of the women as well as their own staff, serves to keep the issues of violence out of sight in the community. Domestic violence drop-in centers more visible within our communities may well be required. Ensuring

138   the safety of the women as well as staff is a considerable challenge to these walk-in centers, but it is one which can and must be met.

Community policing activities, when well conceived and executed, motivate community residents to report criminal activities, such as drug sales, to the police. It is only when community residents decide no longer to tolerate crime and violence and are no longer afraid to call the police that the cycle of crime can be broken. It is now time for community policing programs to work with residents on domestic violence issues as well.

Like domestic violence victims who must squarely confront the issue of their own fear, community residents must be brave enough to call the police when they hear or view domestic violence. Only then will abusers understand that their friends and neighbors have low tolerance for domestic violence. But in many instances, owing to fears of retaliation, community members decide not to risk their own safety to help keep girls and women free from interpersonal violence.

An entire network of concerned citizens and agencies needs to be built. Each component needs to understand his or her role, from the police officer who comes promptly and responds affirmatively, to the employer who does not cave in to the antics of the abuser at the workplace.

Bernice believes that it is only when the community develops an intolerance for domestic violence that violence can be eradicated.

> All the times we had serious fights in that apartment, if I didn't call the police, nobody ever called. Yesterday I was on my way to work and I saw a man beating a woman with a chain. I stopped my car and I went and called the police. What was the outcome, I don't know, but I did call. I will call every time I see it. I don't care who it is, I will not accept it. If I am in my apartment and I hear somebody fighting next door, I am not going to accept it. Don't fight around me. Everyone needs to be like that.

Had her community been better equipped in these ways to reach out to her, to respond to her needs with concern, information, and support, had some agency somewhere provided her with professional counseling to help her escape and recover from the effects of living with severe violence for thirteen years, Bernice thinks the number of years she lived within her own private hell would have been greatly reduced.

And yet all these strategies continue to focus on girls and women, when it is the men who are the batterers in the majority of the cases. Why is battering more prevalent among low-income men? The answer to this question should inform antipoverty policy as well.

CHAPTER NINE

Violence and Poverty: The Causes

> The desire to support wife and children—what motive could be more powerful, or deeply rooted? For it was connected with manhood itself—a man who could not support his family failed in his own conception of manliness.
>
> —VIRGINIA WOOLF, "The Intellectual Status of Women"

Thinking that her story can help shed some light on the link between poverty and domestic violence, I decide to ask Bernice why she thinks Billy turned into an abuser. Immediately she responds that Billy's joblessness was the causative factor.

> All he wanted was to take care of his family. When he went out there and looked for jobs and couldn't get enough money, he got frustrated. He always felt he should have a better job than what he had. These boys want to work and there is no program for them. He would have gone to training. He wants to be responsible for his children.

Bernice tells me that several months ago she and Billy had a conversation about her economic independence.

> He said, "Bernice, that was one of our biggest problems. I felt so useless as a man, because I never could have taken care of you and

*the kids, and here you are, out there doing it by yourself. I don't
even know how to begin apologizing to you for all the things I have
done. That is why I don't try."*

Today, Bernice sees that Billy is a person who has no place in the world.
He feels bad about who he is. "The man is supposed to be the provider
and the strength. He doesn't know who he is and where he is going,
he is only trying to survive." Billy works for a while and then loses or
quits his entry-level factory job. Why is Billy so often unemployed?
When Billy is employed, according to Bernice, the money that he can
make doesn't allow him to get the things he really wants, and he gets
frustrated.

> *He may want to go on vacation, but the money that he makes only
> takes care of his survival needs, and so he works three years and he
> can never go on vacation. He gets frustrated, and he starts to tear
> himself down. He becomes unmotivated, he can't wake up early
> enough in the morning to be on time for work, he doesn't see change
> coming. He never gets ahead. So he gets so tired of not getting ahead
> that he gets depressed and sabotages himself.*

Bernice always recognized that when Billy was unemployed the violence and abuse got worse. The depression, the meanness, and the
anger all escalated. The time when Billy wasn't working was always the
most dangerous time for Bernice.

> *Any time he is unemployed he has low self-esteem, he is frustrated,
> and he has more time on his hands. He is really upset that I'm going
> to leave, I'll meet someone else and want to be with someone else.
> He's very aggressive, he's always close to home when he is unem-
> ployed. He lives as a person who is very depressed, watching me so I
> don't leave. You're not going to leave him when he is at his lowest.
> That has proven to be very dangerous when you leave him at his
> lowest. I did it. When I left Billy for good in 1993, he wasn't
> working. I left him when it was the most dangerous time for me.*

Even when he had a good job there was still abuse, but there was much
less of it.

> One time Billy had a good job for eleven months. I could go out, I
> could have friends, I could dress the way I wanted. When Billy is
> employed, he has more to offer. But the abuse was still there. Now
> he had to control how the money was spent. He always had to be in
> control.

Bernice also agrees that the differential between her success at job training and Billy's lack of accomplishment certainly was a factor contributing to the domestic violence, which did get worse whenever she took
successful steps toward self-sufficiency. She relates an incident that she
thinks illustrates Billy's upset about the differential. Bernice always used
her welfare check to pay the rent. One day she had put the rent money
in the drawer because the landlord wasn't home from work yet. When
she went to pay the rent, however, the money wasn't in the drawer any
longer.

> What were we going to do? I had never been in a position where I
> couldn't pay the rent. I searched all night, and I cried and cried. I
> felt really awful. Then the next day I looked in the drawer and the
> money was sitting right there. Later it dawned on me that Billy had
> taken the money and hid it from me, because he felt bad that I was
> paying the rent. He wanted me to feel bad about it. I thought, he
> must really feel awful to hide the rent money.

Bernice also remembers Billy trying to get ahead by going to truck-
driving school on the weekends while he worked during the week. But
he couldn't keep up and dropped out, while Bernice was sailing
through her own training program.

In the end, Bernice now sees Billy as a victim of domestic violence,
trapped in a rut that he couldn't get out of.

> I never knew that. I thought that they just abused their partners, but
> they have the same isolation, it affects them too. You're so scared
> and isolated and you can't move, and neither can they. We're both
> in prison. I broke out of it and he is still in it.

The author and former welfare recipient Rosemary Bray attributes the
violent rages of her father to the same sense of manly inefficacy.

It took many years for me to understand some of what drove him. Part of his problem stemmed from his own frustrations and bitterness about the hand life had dealt him. Daddy was a man who was born to lead—a company, an organization, at the very least, a family. He was intrinsically a patriarch, hungry for control in a world where black men controlled nothing, not even themselves. I didn't know it then, but it was like being on the set of "A Raisin in the Sun," witness to Walter Lee Younger's evil twin. Manhood for my father, as for Walter Lee, meant providing for his family. Like Walter Lee, Daddy was haunted by the vision of white male affluence he saw only from the periphery.[1]

I have never met a battered woman on welfare who did not agree with Bernice's analysis of the relationship between domestic violence and ability to support one's family. It is now time to fully consider the relationship between violence and poverty. Estimates from the redesigned National Crime Victimization Survey between 1992 and 1996 clearly demonstrate that the rate of intimate violence against women generally decreases as household income levels increase. Households with less than $7,500 in annual income, for example, suffer five times the amount of domestic violence as households with income above $50,000, and those with incomes between $7,500 and $15,000 experience three times the amount of domestic violence as households with income above $50,000.[2]

When Susan Lloyd analyzed the data in her neighborhood survey of 824 women in a low-income Chicago neighborhood by economic class, she also found that women in the lowest income level experienced all forms of abuse at higher levels than women in the highest income group. Women with annual incomes between $2,500 and $7,000 reported almost three times the amount of severe violence of those with income between $13,751 and $27,500, and those with incomes over $27,500.[3] A recent study by the New York City Department of Health on homicides in New York City found that the majority of the murders were committed by husbands or boyfriends, but that the murdered women were disproportionately from the poorest boroughs of the city.[4]

This relationship between violence and income has held true in

144   other surveys in Cambodia, Peru, Chile, and Thailand. In a multilevel model of partner violence in inner-city Baltimore, several neighborhood-level factors, including the rate of unemployment, emerged as predictors of domestic violence. Anecdotal evidence from around the world suggests that violence against women increases as the economic situation of the family deteriorates.[5]

Historically, the battered women's movement has emphasized that battering is embedded in all levels of society, where norms condoning male dominance need to be radically changed to hold men accountable for their violence. The domestic violence movement has avoided discussing battering as a problem in any way related to poverty to avoid its marginalization as an issue, and to further the understanding that domestic abuse is a reflection of the universal norms of a sexist society.[6] Only recently have several scholars argued that the universality thesis focuses attention on white middle-class victims, failing to consider the needs of poor women of color, who are not valued by the dominant society.[7] Since it is clear that there is a higher prevalence of domestic violence within low-income households, the current explanations of domestic violence do not fully explain the overrepresentation of abuse in poor communities. Although domestic violence does cross all class boundaries, open acknowledgment of the high prevalence of domestic violence within poor households might assist in the development of more nuanced or complex theories of domestic violence.[8]

Recently, multiple explanations have been advanced, and many factors may account for the connection between poverty and domestic violence. One obvious simple explanation, of course, is that poor women, lacking financial resources, are unable to escape the violent relationship to the extent that their better-off counterparts can, accounting for larger numbers of women stuck in violence in low-income households. As we have seen, many women such as Bernice may invest more in these relationships, having much more at stake, and perhaps endure more years of violence in the process. Others have suggested that our efforts to eradicate domestic violence may have been more effective to date for middle-class women. The greater stress of unemployment, community violence, and racism have also been cited as factors.[9]

Some analysts believe that low-income men, unable to support their families and dominate them through the paycheck, will attempt to control women by other means. "Men use violence to maintain control over women when the usual forms of power that they have, such as superiority of the wage packet, are missing."[10] This theory however, has been recently undercut by fairly persuasive qualitative evidence that abusers deliberately employ violence to prevent women from becoming economically self-sufficient, suggesting that the differential between the economic power of men and women in these relationships is at the heart of the issue.[11]

Interviews with battered women, and Bernice's story, show that abusers seek to prohibit their partners' employment for the very good reason that they know that if the women had more resources they would leave, or at the workplace they might meet a working man with more money who would be more attractive. It is the woman's economic potential, as compared to that of her male partner, that might be the trigger for the violence. The fewer the economic resources of the male partner, the more intense the response that can be expected. The abuser thus works overtime to maintain the economic imbalance that leans in his favor. As we have seen, women on welfare who have not steadily worked are the perfect matches for extremely low-income men.

Most recently a number of research studies have discovered a correlation between imbalance of resources and domestic violence. In Lisa Brush's Pittsburgh sample, women who had less than a high school diploma or its equivalent reported significantly lower rates of work-related jealousy than those with these credentials.[12] Hotaling and Sugarman found that domestic violence increased when the wife had more education or higher income than her husband.[13] In a sample of 365 women in Arizona, researchers found that total family income per se had no influence on domestic violence, but income disparity did. Violence against women increased as the interspousal income gap closed; the less disparity in income, or the more resources the woman had in relation to her husband, the more frequent and escalated the violence.[14] Analysis of a sample of 102 women in California recently found that receipt of no income from the male partner was significantly correlated with increased relationship abuse within the preceding three months.[15]

Another bit of evidence has recently surfaced that encourages us to focus on the earning capacities of male batterers. In analyzing data from the National Maternal and Infant Health Survey, researchers compared older men who father children with minors to their peers who father

146   children with adult women. They found the men having relationships with adolescents to be less desirable partners, with comparatively less education and lower earning potential. The researchers hypothesize that these men seek younger partners because of their lack of success in the market for adult female partners. The age disparity raises serious concerns about sexual coercion and domestic violence.[16]

In this regard, it is fascinating to take a look at the writings of Olive Schreiner, who worked so hard to secure women's right to work at the beginning of the twentieth century. Schreiner believed that women's economic dependence on men was a kind of prostitution. Where there was true economic equity between the sexes, intimate relationships would become true romantic partnerships based on real attractions and affection alone. The prescience of Schreiner, writing almost ninety years ago about the inevitable backlash, is startling:

> To the male, whenever and wherever he exists in our societies, who depends mainly for his power for procuring the sex relation he desires, not on his power of winning and retaining personal affection, but, on the purchasing power of his possessions, as compared to the poverty of the females of his society, the personal loss would be seriously and at once felt, of any social change which gave to the woman a larger economic independence and therefore greater freedom of sexual choice. . . . A subtle and profound instinct warns him, that with the increased intelligence and economic freedom of woman, he, and such as he, might ultimately be left sexually companionless, the undesirable, the residuary, male old-maid of the human race.[17]

Many of the women in Amina Mama's interviews of one hundred women in inner-city London were assaulted by men who also depended on them.

> This indicates that men continue to dominate women emotionally and physically even when they depend on those women. Indeed, the evidence is that this can be an exacerbating factor. Many women cited the fact that they were working and had some economic independence, as a source

of antagonism. . . . It seems that when women have even a limited material advantage over the men they have relationships with, this in itself may in fact provoke those men to assert their male authority literally with a vengeance, through violence. This dynamic suggests that the frustration felt by men who are unable to conform to patriarchal standards manifests itself in misogynistic behaviour towards the women they live off. Thus we can see that socio-economic jealousy may operate in a way that parallels sexual jealousy and often links up with it.[18]

Looking at the situation in another way, we would also expect to see such a backlash during times of economic and social change. Full acceptance of women in the workplace has surely been hampered by the high rise of male unemployment.[19] Betty Friedan, pointing out instances in which domestic violence escalated in the wake of community dislocation, argues that in times of economic stress women become the scapegoats.[20]

Then along comes welfare reform, insisting that all low-income women must work, and in some instances providing resources, education, training, and other supportive services to them. Welfare reform marks a radical acceleration of this process of social and economic change in the general society and can be expected to cause a backlash in poor neighborhoods. One thoughtful analyst sees how welfare reform puts the low-income abuser in a bind. On one hand, he understands that his partner's working will put the household ahead financially, which would be a good thing. On the other hand, if she works, he fears, she will be out of his control and might leave him. If the abuser lets this latter fear guide his actions, the household will lose welfare benefits and be even poorer than before. Opting for control consigns the family to poverty, and he knows it. From the point of view of the abuser, all the choices are poor, and the conflict within him can cause considerable stress and hostility as the walls close in. This appears to be a convincing psychological explanation for Billy's actions in Bernice's story.[21]

Absent from this analysis, however, is a convincing explanation for the use of violence aimed at intimate partners. One might expect coercion, sabotage, or general turmoil, but why violence? One author postulates that low occupational standing may index a number of other descriptors, including low educational achievement, low self-esteem, lower social skills, and alcohol or drug problems that may contribute toward the use of violence.[22] Based on his many years of interviewing incarcerated males, the psychiatrist James Gilligan identifies the issue of shame that turns to hate and violence. His analysis seems especially persuasive because it integrates the issue of class and provides a convincing rationale for why men turn to violence and stalking, especially after the women leave the relationships.

Gilligan says that batterers experience a "life-death dependency" on their partners and an overwhelming shame because of it. These men do everything they can to make their wives dependent on them, so that the women cannot possibly leave or abandon them. When their wives do leave them, "it intensifies the feelings of shame it causes; it increases the intensity of violence that such shame stimulates":

> The horror of dependency is what causes violence. The emotion that causes the horror of dependency is shame. Men, much more than women, are taught that to want love or care from others is to be passive, dependent, unaggressive and unambitious or, in short, womanly; and that they will be subjected to shaming, ridicule, and disrespect if they appear unmanly in the eyes of others. Women, by contrast, have traditionally been taught that they will be honored if, and only if, they accept a role that restricts them to the relatively passive aim of arranging to be loved by men and to depend on men for their social and economic status, forgoing or severely limiting or disguising activity, ambition, independence, and initiative of their own.

Shame, which consists of a deficiency of self-love, says Gilligan, causes hate, which becomes violence, usually directed at other people. Given the horror of dependency in the United States, especially dependency of men, is it any wonder that we have so much male violence? The economic needs of men must be gratified. By not helping men to meet these needs, we shame them for having the desire that all people have. To prevent domestic violence, then, we must work to eliminate relative poverty and race discrimination.[23]

The 1996 killing of Galina Komar in Queens, New York, graphically illustrates this sense of shame. Ms. Komar's ex-boyfriend, who had severely abused her in the past, came to her place of employment and shot her with a .44 magnum. He then turned the gun on himself. Both died instantly. Ms. Komar's mother told the press that when her daughter left her partner, he said, "I don't have a job. I have nothing to lose. I'm going to kill myself and everybody."[24]

Clearly we have a way to go to unravel the complex issue of violence and poverty. More research is certainly in order. We need to document episodes of violence to see if there is a correlation with women's attempts to work. Also, we need to interview women's partners to obtain a better sense of the stresses and conflicts that are fueling men's anger and violence in low-income communities. This is not in any way to condone domestic violence or to deny that in our society there have been powerful cultural messages that have supported male dominance over women; but by moving toward a more nuanced view of batterers, the battered women's movement stands a better chance of being able to work with those communities and activists who feel loyalty to their abusers out of solidarity to the community and sympathy for the disadvantages they face. The issue of domestic violence and welfare forces us now to begin to synthesize theories of domestic violence causation.[25]

Until we have a better understanding of the reasons for the higher prevalence of domestic violence in poor households, we will be powerless to craft truly effective interventions or work to prevent it. As for welfare reform, Bernice's story tells us enough of what we need to know: the process of achieving equality and self-sufficiency may inadvertently put some poor women at greater risk of violence.

The article on Michelle Crawford on the front page of the 29 April 1999 New York Times is positively ominous. The former welfare recipient is pictured telling her successful welfare-to-work story to the entire Wisconsin Legislature in January. After ten years on welfare, she is now a machine operator, and her family is off welfare. Reporter Jason DeParle went behind the hype to discover the real story.

The real story is Ms. Crawford's husband of two years, a recovering drug addict who is an aspiring minister. At least four times last year Mr. Crawford badly injured his wife through serious physical attacks. As recently as a year ago Ms. Crawford was hospitalized for a nervous breakdown. DeParle interviewed Mr. Crawford, who worries that his

150   role as the breadwinner is being usurped. "I don't like it, because I'm the man of the house," he told the reporter. He also angrily complained that his wife had failed to tell the legislative audience about his contribution to her success. "I pulled that lady in there out of a lot of rough stuff," he said. "Don't kick me to the curb, like 'I did it all by myself.' "

DeParle recounts that Ms. Crawford's co-workers resent her celebrity, and closer to home her husband chafes at her prominence. "I'm trying to go straight in the Lord," he said. But his anger flared just a moment later, when he noticed that in her defining hour, Ms. Crawford "didn't say nothing about me."[26]

It doesn't look like it will be possible to eliminate women's poverty without doing something about the pressing needs of the other half of the equation: low-income men.

Epilogue

We have proved, sitting eating, sitting talking, that we can
add to the treasury of moments. We are not slaves bound to
suffer incessantly unrecorded petty blows on our bent backs.
We are not sheep either, following a master. We are creators.
We too have made something that will join the innumerable
congregations of past time. We too, as we put on our hats
and push open the door, stride not into chaos, but into a
world that our own force can subjugate and make part of
the illumined and everlasting road.

—VIRGINIA WOOLF, *The Waves*

The years 1997–98 brought several new developments for Bernice and
her family. Bernice's mother was diagnosed as a paranoid schizophrenic
who will eventually need institutionalization. At her school, nine-year-
old Jessica was diagnosed with a learning disability, the result of trau-
matization from violence and stalking. She doesn't listen well or take in
new information, and now, in the fourth grade, she hasn't been able to
learn to read. Jessica continues to daydream and disassociate. According
to Bernice, neither the therapy nor the special education classes seems
to be making much of an improvement at the moment.

Bernice says that Jessica's teachers believe that she has the potential
and that she needs to be making more of an effort. For this reason, her
teachers are impatient with Jessica. As a result, Jessica is unhappy at
school.

152   Bernice tries to motivate Jessica about the future. She tells her she will go to college, get a job, and have her own place.

> She says, "Oh no, Mommy, we are going to stay together forever."
> Her reaction was so strong that I just said, "Okay, Jessica, it's okay." She is still so frightened. She has all these baby dolls. She brings me two or three of her dolls every night and says, "Mommy, they are going to protect you while you sleep."

Bernice says Jessica still has nightmares. She dreams she is being chased or is falling. When Jessica tells her about her dreams, Bernice says, it is almost like talking with another battered woman. Every time that Bernice has to leave Jessica with a babysitter, Jessica worries whether her mother is going to come back and get her.

Clearly, Jessica is depressed.

> I have to motivate Jessica every single day. I tell her she is going to have a really good day. Then when she gets in the car after school she says, you were right, it was a good day. But if I forget to tell her these things, she doesn't have a good day. I feel like I have my own little Life Skills class in my home. Jessica sees me talking to myself in the mirror. I have this little saying, Bernice, it's okay today. She gets in front of the mirror and says, "It's okay today, Jessica." And she also chants, "If you don't love you, nobody else will." Jessica copes very well for someone who is so fearful. But her state of mind takes away from her learning.

Now thirteen, Little Billy is flourishing in school. And Bernice says he sees a way out for himself. He wants to go away to college. Little Billy desires to become a nurse, and he asks whether as a nurse he will be able to support himself and live on his own. Little Billy loves his father and wishes to protect him, but he also wants to have a life of his own. Bernice says he is in conflict with these two emotions.

> I try to solve the conflict with him. He asks me questions, like, Mom, do you think I am going to be a good man? Do you think I am going to be able to take care of you? That I am going to have a good life? I talk to him all the time, and I tell him that he is a

*special kind of kid, there is no one else in the world like him. That
your father is only one part of you, and all these other aspects of you
will grow and become bigger than what you have for your father. It
happened to me and it will happen for you.*

*He looks at me with such relief, because his relationship with
his father is such a big thing for him, bigger than him. When I talk
to him, I let him know that I am the representation for him of a
whole new life. This life is your life, and it is a bigger component
than your dad's life.*

But will Billy let Little Billy go into the wider world? Although Billy is
starting to become uneasy with his own son's surpassing him, Bernice
believes that he will.

*He is going to let him go. He doesn't want little Billy to run away
from him like I did. He will do it right this time. Billy always talks
about how I ran away from him. I always have to respond, "You
forced me to run away from you, and you will force other people to
run from you if you don't change." I think he is listening.*

Bernice has restructured how she is raising her children.

*My children are allowed to tell me they don't like something. We
apologize to each other. I thought about what I would have liked
when I was a little girl, and so I have tried to set that world up for
my children. I want to know what they think, and I want to know
if I have done something that hurts them. Because nobody ever
checked in with me.*

Bernice is teaching the children how to compromise, how to get along
with other people and other children. She has taught them not to fight
with other children—not to be silent or cowardly, but how to mediate.
Billy still encourages the children to fight and confront other children.
When they refuse, Billy gets mad and doesn't talk to them.

And what of Bernice herself? In January 1998 Bernice started working toward a college degree in psychology by taking two courses on
Tuesday and Thursday evenings, one in algebra and the other in criminal justice.

*I've studied human behavior, now I want the theory. I have a job,
but now I want the office, the briefcase, the title, and I want that
house, the house with the white picket fence. I want the American
dream.*

The college experience has been upsetting. Bernice flunked the first
algebra test, and the instructor suggested that she drop the class. Bernice
refused and instead got a special math tutor. But she says that her ability
to retain new information is limited. "I feel like when I am in the
classroom I can understand what the instructor is talking about, but the
minute I walk out, it is all gone. In the past, once I understood something, it was in there. I feel like I am totally blocked." Bernice didn't
expect this. "I am totally lost. I go to school an hour and a half early to
prepare my mind, to get used to the setting, the environment. Something is wrong." After about forty hours of study, Bernice got Bs on
both her midterm exams. But she remains concerned about a deteriora-
tion in her cognitive abilities.

Bernice's criminal justice teacher has also made a big point about
Bernice's emotional approach to issues instead of relying on facts to
marshall her arguments. So Bernice is struggling to apply the facts to
the rules of the statutes and court cases, as opposed to following her
gut or emotional reactions. This task, too, is akin to the challenges she
first found when she began work.

The entire experience, however, makes Bernice feel like a child who
has everything to learn. As a matter of fact, although Bernice appears to
be moving ahead in building her new life, what she often feels like is
an adolescent who has everything to try out and experience. Only now
does she understand how totally isolated she was as a teen and a young
adult. Because she believes she is a person who lacks so many basic
experiences and knowledge, Bernice has yet to trust her gut feelings or
her own instinctive reactions to life's situations. Not being able to trust
in one's own judgment is truly exhausting.

☙

*"Mommy," Jessica asked when she heard about this book, "is the
book going to be about us? What did we do?" I began to talk about
domestic violence, and she says, "Is that important?" I replied, "It*

is important, Jessica. Some people think what we did was very impor-
tant."

Bernice hopes that the book about Jessica's mother will serve as a guide-
post to the creation of Jessica's own life.

And so, all the secrets are out. We conclude "Bernice's Book" with
the hope that it will help us as a nation to create the preconditions that
will prevent the Bernices of this world from having to make this long
and difficult journey out of the dark, and to enable all of us to better
support women like Bernice when they do.

Bernice is continually searching out new resources, mentors, and
role models for the woman and parent she wants to be.

> *Sometimes I think there is just the three of us, that is all the world*
> *consists of, just us three. That is not a good way to live, or to have*
> *your children imitate anything like that. I would like to see how*
> *other people live, to educate me. I would like to know how other*
> *people live.*

I ask Bernice, what does she mean about wanting to know how other
people live? She responds by talking about wanting to hear about how
to have an intimate relationship among equals, how two people can
respect one another, have a disagreement, but not have it develop into
a confrontation.

> *I think that men and women can have an argument and it can not*
> *go to the point where they have a fight. I don't think that you have*
> *to be afraid to voice your opinion. I have never seen it happen. I want*
> *to know how they do it. I don't know anybody who is like that.*
>
> *I want some confirmation. I want to see it. Not so much that*
> *I want to see it, but I want to be a part of it. I want to have that*
> *nice little house on that block where people don't fight. I read an*
> *article about this nice little block, but there was one house where the*
> *man was abusing his partner. So all the women on the block waited*
> *for him to go to work, and they went down there and talked to his*
> *wife. And when they would hear them fighting, they would call the*

·

police, every time. And the police came. Finally, he got tired of it and left his wife.

I want to see it, I want to be a part of it, and I am striving for that. That is why I go to school and that is why I work. I want to live on that block.

Notes

PROLOGUE

1. Charles Murray, *Losing Ground: American Social Policy, 1950–1980* (New York: Basic Books, 1984), 220.

2. Lawrence M. Mead, *The New Politics of Poverty: The Nonworking Poor in America* (New York: Basic Books, 1992), 24.

3. Dan Quayle and Diane Medved, *The American Family* (New York: Harper-Collins, 1996), 280; Barbara Dafoe Whitehead, "Dan Quayle Was Right," *Atlantic Monthly*, April 1993, 62.

4. Ruth Sidel, *Keeping Women and Children Last* (New York: Penguin Books, 1996), 183–84.

5. Kathryn Edin and Laura Lein, *Making Ends Meet: How Single Mothers Survive Welfare and Low Wage Work* (New York: Russell Sage Foundation, 1997).

6. Newspaper columnists had a heyday on this topic. Here are two typical examples. "Interpreting welfare reform as mean to the poor is like interpreting parental discipline as cruel to children. In both cases, the point is not to hurt but to help—by teaching responsibility and self-control to people who have not yet learned it" (Stephen Chapman, "Target Practice: Conservatives Are Being Attacked by All Sides for 'Trampling on the Poor,' but in the End They Will Be Vindicated," *Chicago Tribune*, 24 September 1995). "The second is behavioral poverty, [which] includes a cluster of pathological behaviors: out-of-wedlock births, prolonged welfare dependence . . ." (Joan Beck, "Nation Must Stem the Tide of Births Out of Wedlock," *New Orleans Times-Picayune*, 6 March 1993, sec. B).

7. Sidel, *Keeping Women and Children Last*, 183.

8. Heidi Hartmann and Roberta Spalter-Roth, "Reducing Welfare's Stigma: Policies That Build upon Commonalities among Women," *Connecticut Law Review* 26 (1994): 901, 909; Rebecca M. Blank, *It Takes a Nation: A New Agenda for Fighting Poverty* (New York: Russell Sage Foundation, 1997), 257–66.

158

9. Mimi Abramovitz, *Regulating the Lives of Women: Social Welfare Policy from Colonial Times to the Present* (Boston: South End Press, 1988), 355; Martha Fineman, *The Neutered Mother, the Sexual Family, and Other Twentieth Century Tragedies* (New York: Routledge Press, 1995), 125.

10. U.S. Public Law 104–193, 104th Cong., 2d sess., 30 July 1996.

11. For an in-depth discussion of the needless polarization of the welfare reform debate, see Michael Tomasky, *Left for Dead: The Life, Death, and Possible Resurrection of Progressive Politics in America* (New York: Free Press, 1996), 96–117. Tomasky convincingly argues that the liberals, who refused to discuss the behavior and morals of the poor, ceded the entire debate to the conservatives.

12. Jody Raphael, "Prisoners of Abuse: Domestic Violence and Welfare Receipt" (report, Chicago, 1996), 6–10; Catherine T. Kenney and Karen R. Brown, "Report from the Front Lines: The Impact of Violence on Poor Women" (report, New York, 1996), 15–21.

13. Stacey Plichta, "Violence and Abuse: Implications for Women's Health," in *Women's Health: The Commonwealth Fund Survey* (Baltimore: Johns Hopkins University Press, 1996), 237–70; Jody Raphael and Richard M. Tolman, "Trapped by Poverty/Trapped by Abuse" (report, Chicago, 1997), 21. The Commonwealth Fund survey estimates that 3.2 percent of women married or living with a partner are victims of severe spouse abuse. This survey does not include women abused by noncohabiting partners. A recent national sample measuring violence from noncohabiting partners finds a comparable percentage of assaults; see Patricia Tjaden and Nancy Thoennes, "Stalking in America: Findings from the National Violence against Women Survey" (report, Denver, 1997), 1–25.

14. Jerry Silverman, U.S. Department of Health and Human Services, conversation with author, 20 July 1999.

15. Sylvia Walby, *Theorizing Patriarchy* (Oxford: Blackwell, 1990), 142–43; Joan Meier, "Domestic Violence, Character, and Social Change in the Welfare Reform Debate," *Law and Policy* 19, no. 2 (1997): 52–54. See also Stephanie Riger and Maryann Krieglstein, "The Impact of Welfare Reform on Men's Violence against Women," *American Journal of Community Psychology*, forthcoming.

16. R. Emerson Dobash and Russell Dobash, *Women, Violence, and Social Change* (New York: Routledge, 1992), 52–54.

17. Meier, "Domestic Violence," 219, 232–37. Meier explores the reasons why most antipoverty advocates have been reluctant to admit that the behavior of low-income people might contribute to their own poverty, as they criticize the conservatives' obsession with family values and individual character of the poor as a reflection of class, gender, and racial bias. Meier also provides an in-depth discussion of what this more complex view of domestic violence might consist, moving away from the simplistic, stereotypical paradigm of battering.

18. Jill Nelson, *Straight, No Chaser: How I Became a Grown-up Black Woman* (New York: Putnam Penguin, 1997), 12, 18.

1. The author formally interviewed Bernice Hampton face-to-face approximately twelve times between 1995 and 1999. All comments and quotes from Bernice Hampton in this work derive from these taped interviews.

2. Jason DeParle, "Shrinking Welfare Rolls Leave Record High Share of Minorities," New York Times, 27 July 1998, sec. A.

3. Beth E. Richie, Compelled to Crime: The Gender Entrapment of Battered Black Women (New York: Routledge, 1996), 135.

4. Ibid., 139, 147.

5. Nelson, Straight, No Chaser, 11.

7. Mary Field Belenky et al., Women's Ways of Knowing: The Development of Self, Voice, and Mind (New York: Basic Books, 1986), 33.

7. Ibid., 34.

8. Ibid., 159–60.

9. Lyn Mikel Brown and Carol Gilligan, Meeting at the Crossroads: Women's Psychology and Girls' Development (Cambridge, Mass.: Harvard University Press, 1992), 214.

10. Richie, Compelled to Crime, 147.

11. Jill Gerston, "Television: Big Hospitals, Strong Women, Prime Time: A Former Moll Flanders Joins the Surgical Staff," New York Times, 15 February 1998, sec. 2.

12. These comments were made by William Curcio in a presentation at the University of Michigan School of Social Work on 7 November 1996.

13. Jody Raphael, "Domestic Violence: Telling the Untold Welfare-to-Work Story" (report, Chicago, 1995), 1–6.

14. Plichta, "Violence and Abuse," 237–70, n. 14.

15. Silverman conversation, 20 July 1999.

16. William Curcio, "The Passaic County Study of AFDC Recipient in a Welfare-to-Work Program: A Preliminary Analysis" (report, Paterson, N.J., 1997), 3.

17. McCormack Institute and Center for Survey Research, "In Harm's Way? Domestic Violence, AFDC Receipt and Welfare Reform in Massachusetts" (report, Boston, 1997), 17.

18. Susan Lloyd, "The Effects of Domestic Violence on Women's Employment," Law and Policy 19, no. 2 (1997): 153.

19. Dan Jones and Associates, "Domestic Violence Incidence and Prevalence Study" (report, Salt Lake City, 1997), 13–14. See also Sheila B. Haennicke et al., "Trapped by Poverty, Trapped by Abuse," Supplement I (report, Chicago, 1998), 6, for a detailed breakdown of domestic violence statistics by welfare qualifiers and nonqualifiers.

20. Plitchta, "Violence and Abuse," 237–70.

21. Ellen Bassuk et al., "The Characteristics and Needs of Sheltered Home-

160   less and Low-Income Mothers," *Journal of the American Medical Association* 276, no. 8 (1966): 643.

22. Amy Salomon, Shari S. Bassuck, and Margaret G. Brooks, "Patterns of Welfare Use among Poor and Homeless Women," *American Journal of Orthopsychiatry* 66, no. 4 (1996): 516–24.

23. Richard M. Tolman and Daniel Rosen, "Domestic Violence in the Lives of Welfare Recipients: Implications for the Family Violence Option," paper presented at the Association for Public Policy Analysis and Management Conference, New York City, October 1998, 12–13.

24. Lisa D. Brush, "Battering, Traumatic Stress, and Welfare-to-Work Transition," *Violence against Women*, forthcoming.

25. Amanda Barusch et al., "Understanding Families with Multiple Barriers to Self-Sufficiency" (report, Salt Lake City, 1999), 2.

CHAPTER TWO

1. Raphael, "Prisoners," 6.

2. Letter from Karen R. Brown to author, 17 November 1995.

3. Molly Robertson, telephone interview with Helene Marcy, 3 August 1999.

4. These anecdotes were shared by Sylvia Benson in a taped interview with the author on 24 February 1997.

5. Author interviews, 3 May 1996.

6. Center for Social Work Research, "Good Cause Temporary Waivers and Modifications for Victims of Domestic Violence" (report, San Antonio, 1999), 14.

7. Author interview, 3 May 1996.

8. Author interview, 31 October 1997.

9. Horizon Research Services, "Focus Group Participants: Clients of Women's Employment Network" (report, Columbia, 1996), 31.

10. Author interview with Kathy Vaslovik, 10 September 1998.

11. Horizon Research, "Focus Group," 24.

12. McCormack Institute, "In Harm's Way," 30.

13. Virginia Department of Social Services, "A Summary of Responses from Local Departments of Social Services to a Questionnaire on Domestic Violence" (report, Richmond, Virginia, n.d.), 2–3.

14. Jeff Kunerth, "She Got a Job and His Abuse," *Orlando Sentinel*, 21 December 1997.

15. Christine Owens, conversation with author, 21 January 1998.

16. Curcio, "Passaic County," 3.

17. McCormack Institute, "In Harm's Way?," 25.

18. Jessica Pearson, Nancy Thoennes, and Esther Ann Griswold, "Child

Support and Domestic Violence: The Victims Speak Out," *Violence against Women*
5, no. 4 (1999): 439.

19. Stephanie Riger et al., "Obstacles to Employment of Welfare Recipients
with Abusive Partners" (report, Chicago, 1998), 14–15.

20. Ohio Domestic Violence Network, "Study on Economic Status of
Women in Domestic Violence Populations: January 1997" (report, Columbus,
1997); Melanie Shepard and Ellen Pence, "The Effects of Battering on the Employment Status of Women" (report, Duluth, n.d.), 5.

21. Susan Lloyd and Nina Taluc, "The Effects of Male Violence on Female
Employment," *Violence against Women* 5, no. 4 (1999): 376.

22. Brush, "Battering," 7–10.

23. Angela Browne, Amy Salomon, and Shari S. Bassuk, "The Impact of
Recent Partner Violence on Poor Women's Capacity to Maintain Work," *Violence
against Women* 5, no. 4 (1999): 410–23.

CHAPTER THREE

1. James Gilligan, *Violence: Our Deadly Epidemic and Its Causes* (New York: Putnam, 1996), 230–31, 233.

2. Joan Haldeman, interview with author, 30 September 1997.

3. Jacquelyn C. Campbell et al., "The Influence of Abuse on Pregnancy
Intention," *Women's Health Issues* 5, no. 4 (1995): 219–20.

4. Joyce Abma, Anne Driscoll, and Kristin Moore, "Young Women's Degree of Control over First Intercourse: An Exploratory Analysis," *Family Planning
Perspectives* 30, no. 1 (1998): 14–17.

5. Gina M. Wingood and Ralph J. DiClemente, "The Effects of an Abusive
Primary Partner on the Condom Use and Sexual Negotiation Practices of African-American Women," *American Journal of Public Health* 87, no. 6 (1997): 1017.

6. Lynn Phillips, "The Girls Report: What We Know and Need to Know
about Growing Up Female" (report, New York, 1998), 38.

7. Kim S. Miller, Leslie F. Clark, and Janet S. Moore, "Sexual Initiation
with Older Male Partners and Subsequent HIV Risk Behavior," *Family Planning
Perspectives* 29, no. 5 (1997): 213–14.

8. The data is contained in Child Trends, Inc., "New Research, Latest
State-Level Data Available on Teen Sexual Behavior, Pregnancy and Births" (report, Washington, D.C., 1997), 1.

9. Judith S. Musick, *Young, Poor, and Pregnant: The Psychology of Teenage Motherhood*
(New Haven, Conn.: Yale University Press, 1993), 59–99, 116.

10. Aline T. Geronimus, "Teenage Childbearing and Personal Responsibility: An Alternative View," *Political Science Quarterly* 112, no. 3 (1997): 425.

11. Kristin Luker, *Dubious Conceptions: The Politics of Teenage Pregnancy* (Cambridge, Mass.: Harvard University Press, 1996), 192.

12. Rebekah Levine Coley and P. Lindsay Chase-Lansdale, "Adolescent

162   Pregnancy and Parenthood: Recent Evidence and Future Directions," *American Psychologist* 53, no. 2 (1998): 157.

CHAPTER FOUR

1. Caroline Wolf Harlow, "Female Victims and Violent Crime" (report, Washington, D.C., 1991), 5.

2. Aysan Sev'er, "Recent or Imminent Separation and Intimate Violence against Women: A Conceptual Overview and Some Canadian Examples," *Violence against Women* 3, no. 6 (1997): 569.

3. Tjaden and Thoennes, "Stalking in America," 2–16.

4. Susan A. Wilt, Susan M. Illman, and Maia Brody Field, "Female Homicide Victims in New York City, 1990–1994" (report, New York City, 1997), 16.

5. Sev'er, "Recent or Imminent Separation," 569.

6. Angela Browne and Shari S. Bassuk, "Intimate Violence in the Lives of Homeless and Poor Housed Women: Prevalence and Patterns in an Ethnically Diverse Sample," *American Journal of Orthopsychiatry* 67, no. 2 (1997): 272.

7. Author interview, 16 May 1996.

8. Kate Ginn and Barbara Davies, "My Undying Love for Man Who Shot Me," *Daily Mail*, 12 November 1997.

9. David Simon, Joe Nawrozki, and Gary Cohn, "Loving Father's Tragic Solution," *Baltimore Sun*, 18 September 1995, sec. A.

10. John D. McKinnon, "Battered Wife Challenges Denial of Jobless Benefits," *Wall Street Journal*, 30 July 1997.

11. Peter G. Jaffe and David A. Wolfe, *Children of Battered Women* (Newbury Park, Calif.: Sage, 1990), 20–21, 71–73.

12. Judith Lennett, "Children of Domestic Violence" (report, Boston, 1996), 13–14.

13. Patti Davis, interview with author, 10 September 1998.

CHAPTER FIVE

1. Richard Davenport-Hines, *Auden* (New York: Pantheon Books, 1995), 1–2.

2. Interviews with domestic violence survivors held by the author in Salt Lake City, Utah, 17 May 1996.

3. Belenky et al., *Women's Ways*, 81.

4. "Pat's Story" (report, Salt Lake City, 1996), 2.

5. Horizon Research Services, "Focus Group Participants: Social Workers and Employers" (report, Columbia, 1996), 24.

6. Catherine Kirkwood, *Leaving Abusive Partners: From the Scars of Survival to the Wisdom of Change* (London: Sage, 1993), 117.

7. Rebekah Levin, author interview, June 1998.

8. Letter to author, 18 May 1998.

9. Sylvia Benson, interview with author, 24 February 1997.

10. Letter from a domestic violence survivor in Colorado Springs, Colorado, 1 January 1995.

11. Letter from a domestic violence survivor in Columbus, Ohio, 14 February 1997.

12. Mary Ann Dutton, *Empowering and Healing the Battered Woman: A Model for Assessment and Intervention* (New York: Springer, 1992), 52, 54–55.

13. Judith Herman, *Trauma and Recovery* (New York: Basic Books, 1992), 127.

14. Patricia A. Murphy, "Recovering from the Effects of Domestic Violence: Implications for Welfare Reform Policy," *Law and Policy* 19, no. 2 (1997): 172–73. See also Dutton, *Empowering and Healing*, for a comprehensive description of the various posttraumatic stress disorder symptoms.

15. Diego Gambetta, "Primo Levi's Plunge: A Case against Suicide," *New York Times*, 7 August 1999, sec. A. As Levi was recovering from a prostate operation, on an antidepressant, and had complained of dizziness, Gambetta believes Levi's death was most likely accidental, despite the depression he suffered.

16. Evan Stark and Anne Flitcraft, "Personal Power and Institutional Victimization: Treating the Dual Trauma of Woman's Battering," in *Post Traumatic Therapy and Victims of Violence*, ed. Frank M. Ochberg (New York: Brunner/Mazel, 1988), 120.

17. Bassuk et al., "Characteristics and Needs," 643–44.

18. Browne et al., "Impact of Recent Partner Violence," 412, 417.

19. Tolman and Rosen, "Domestic Violence," 14–15.

20. Sandra Danziger et al., "Barriers to the Employment of Welfare Recipients" (paper presented at the Association for Public Policy Analysis and Management Conference, New York City, October 1998), 24.

21. Brush, "Battering," 8–10.

22. Stark and Flitcraft, "Personal Power," 120; Dutton, *Empowering and Healing*, 64.

23. Browne et al., "Characteristics and Needs," 644.

24. Salamon et al., "Patterns of Welfare Use," 519.

25. Curcio, "Passaic County," 6–7.

26. Tolman and Rosen, "Domestic Violence," 14.

27. Danziger et al., "Barriers to Employment," 12–13.

28. Since its introduction by the anthropologist Oscar Lewis in 1968, the concept of the "culture of poverty" has caused controversy. Lewis's theory held that poor communities adapt their culture to outward circumstances and that once it comes into existence, the culture perpetuates itself from generation to generation through its effects on children (Oscar Lewis, "The Culture of Poverty," in *On Understanding Poverty* [New York: Basic Books, 1968], 188). In recent years the term "underclass" has gained greater currency, but the con-

164   cept retains its grip in various analyses, such as those of William Julius Wilson, *The Truly Disadvantaged: The Inner City, the Underclass, and Public Policy* (Chicago: University of Chicago Press, 1987).

29. Thomas J. Kane, "Giving Back Control: Long-Term Poverty and Motivation," *Social Science Review* 61, no. 3 (1987): 406, 416.

30. Mead, *The New Politics*, 24, 145.

31. Denise J. Gelinas, "The Persisting Negative Effects of Incest," *Psychiatry* 46, no. 4 (1983): 322.

32. Patricia A. Murphy, *A Career and Life Planning Guide for Women Survivors: Making the Connections Workbook* (Delray Beach, Fla.: St. Lucie Press, 1995), 33–51.

33. Herman, *Trauma*, 35.

34. Murphy, *Career Guide*, 235.

35. Interview with a survivor of domestic violence, 17 May 1996.

36. Carolyn G. Heilbrun, *Writing a Woman's Life* (New York: Norton, 1998), 118.

37. Leslie Lebowitz, Mary R. Harvey, and Judith Lewis Herman, "A Stage-by-Dimension Model of Recovery from Sexual Trauma," *Journal of Interpersonal Violence* 8, no. 3 (1993): 379–82.

38. Dutton, *Empowering and Healing*, 132.

39. Elizabeth A. Stanko, *Intimate Intrusions: Women's Experience of Male Violence* (London: Unwin Hyman, 1985), 73.

40. Dutton, *Empowering and Healing*, 82. See also Belenky et al., *Women's Ways*, 160.

41. Heilbrun, *Writing*, 121.

42. Lori L. Heise, "Violence against Women: An Integrated, Ecological Framework," *Violence against Women* 4, no. 3 (1998): 279.

43. Gilligan, *Violence*, 45.

44. Tamar Lewin, "Americans Are Firmly Attached to Traditional Roles for Sexes, Poll Finds," *New York Times*, 27 March 1996.

45. Richard Morin and Megan Rosenfeld, "With More Equity, More Sweat: Poll Shows Sexes Agree on Pros and Cons of New Roles," *Washington Post*, 22 March 1998, sec. A.

46. Kimberle Williams Crenshaw, "Mapping the Margins: Intersectionality, Identity Politics, and Violence against Women of Color," in *The Public Nature of Private Violence* (New York: Routledge, 1994), 103.

47. Richie, *Compelled to Crime*, 56.

48. Nelson, *Straight, No Chaser*, 157.

49. Valli Kanuha, "Domestic Violence, Racism, and the Battered Women's Movement in the United States," in *Future Interventions with Battered Women and Their Families* (Thousand Oaks, Calif.: Sage, 1996), 44.

50. Clarence Page, *Showing My Color* (New York: HarperCollins, 1996), 106.

51. Walby, *Theorizing Patriarchy*, 76. See also Dorothy E. Roberts, who argues

that the history of slavery has led policy makers to devalue black women's role in the home and therefore, seeing them as unfit mothers, do not think twice about requiring welfare mothers to leave young children to go to work ("The Value of Black Mothers' Work," *Connecticut Law Review* 26 [1994]: 871, 874–75).

52. Richie, *Compelled to Crime*, 142.

53. Murphy, "Recovering," 177, quoting Diana Russell, *Sexual Exploitation: Rape, Child Sexual Abuse, and Workplace Harassment* (Beverly Hills, Calif.: Sage, 1984).

54. Farah A. Ibrahim and Edwin L. Herr, "Battered Women: A Development Life-Career Counseling Perspective," *Journal of Counseling and Development* 65, no. 5 (1987): 247.

CHAPTER SIX

1. A recent interchange on an Internet list serve revealed that it is very common for both the noncustodial father and the mother to file Earned Income Tax Credit (EITC) claims. The legitimate claimant is the parent who lived with the child for more than half the year. Although an appeal can be made when the mother's claim is denied, the challenge has the effect of getting the noncustodial parent in trouble with the IRS, which can put the mother in danger from the father of her children. Reprisals from an abuser may prevent some low-income women from claiming the benefits to which they are entitled under the EITC. www.iwpr.org, 5 May 1999.

CHAPTER SEVEN

1. Rebecca Blank, *It Takes a Nation*, 18.

2. Susan Lloyd, "Effects of Domestic Violence," 142.

3. Curcio, "Passaic County," 3.

4. Lisa Brush, "Family Violence and Control as Obstacles to Self-Sufficiency: Perceptions of Rapid Attachment Participants in Allegheny County, Final Report #2" (Pittsburgh, 1998), 44.

5. U.S. House Committee on Ways and Means. *Contract with America— Welfare Reform*, 104th Cong., 1st sess., 20 January 1995, 141–77.

6. David Blankenhorn, *Fatherless America: Confronting Our Most Urgent Social Problem* (New York: Basic Books, 1995), 19.

7. David Popenoe, *Life without Father: Compelling New Evidence That Fatherhood and Marriage Are Indispensable for the Good of Children and Society* (New York: Free Press, 1996), 192.

8. Sidel, *Women and Children Last*, 183.

9. Blank, *It Takes a Nation*, 37, 39–40.

10. Laura Duberstein Lindberg et al., "Age Differences between Minors Who Give Birth and Their Adult Partners," *Family Planning Perspectives* 29, no. 2 (1997): 63–66.

11. Frank L. Mott, "When Is a Father Really Gone? Paternal-Child Contact in Father-Absent Homes," *Demography* 27, no. 4 (1990): 511–13, 514.

12. Brush, "Battering," 6.

13. Katherine S. Newman, No Shame in My Game: The Working Poor in the Inner City (New York: Knopf and the Russell Sage Foundation, 1999), 198.

14. Teresa L. Amott, "Black Women and AFDC: Making Entitlement out of Necessity," in Women, the State, and Welfare (Madison: University of Wisconsin Press, 1990), 286–87. See also Ann Shola Orlogg, "Gender and the Social Rights of Citizenship: The Comparative Analysis of Gender Relations and Welfare States," American Sociological Review 58, no. 3 (1993): 303–28.

15. Mimi Abramovitz, Regulating the Lives of Women, 355.

16. Fineman, The Neutered Mother, 125.

17. See Monica McWilliams, who argues that in societies under stress, including war-torn areas, domestic violence appears to be maintained longer by the perpetrators and endured longer by victims, because the victims cannot rely on formal and informal helping mechanisms that have collapsed ("Violence against Women in Societies under Stress," in Rethinking Violence against Women [Thousand Oaks, Calif.: Sage, 1998], 138).

18. Mrs. A. Ferris, "When It Pays Not to Work," letter to the editor of the Daily Telegraph, 15 December 1997.

19. Walby, Theorizing Patriarchy, 58, 83.

20. Sylvia Chant, "Gender and Tourism Employment in Mexico and the Phillipines," in Gender, Work, and Tourism (London: Routledge, 1997), 164.

21. Abigail J. Stewart, "Discovering the Meaning of Work," in The Experience and Meaning of Work in Women's Lives (Hillsdale, N.J.: Lawrence Erlbaum Associates, 1990), 262.

22. Letter from Karen R. Brown to author, 17 November 1995.

23. Betty Friedan, The Feminine Mystique (New York: Dell, 1963), 322.

24. Newman, No Shame, 104.

25. John Friedmann, Empowerment: The Politics of Alternative Development (Oxford: Blackwell, 1992), 67–68.

26. Martha C. Nussbaum, Sex and Social Justice (New York: Oxford University Press, 1999), 41, 43.

27. Malcolm Gladwell, "Six Degrees of Lois Weisberg," New Yorker, 11 (January, 1999), 62.

CHAPTER EIGHT

1. Rosemary L. Bray, Unafraid of the Dark (New York: Random House, 1998), 273–74.

2. Brook A. Masters, "Mother Slain a Day after Seeking Help," Washington Post, 28 May 1998, sec. A.

3. Lloyd, "Effects of Domestic Violence," 159.

4. The Family Violence Option can be found at Section 492(a)(B)(7) of Title 1, Temporary Assistance to Needy Families.

5. Jenny Wittner, interview with author, 5 November 1996.

6. Murphy, "Recovering," 176−78.

7. Jody Raphael and Sheila Haennicke, "Keeping Battered Women Safe Through the Welfare-to-Work Journey: How Are We Doing? A Report on the Implementation of Policies for Battered Women in State Temporary Assistance for Needy Families (TANF) Programs," (report, Chicago, 1999), 21−31.

8. Jody Raphael, "The Family Violence Option: An Early Assessment," *Violence against Women* 5, no. 4 (1999): 463−64.

9. Tracy Cooley et al., "Safety and Self-Support: The Challenge of Welfare Reform for Victims of Domestic Abuse" (report, Bangor, 1997), 5.

10. Confidential interview with author, 3 March 1996.

11. Pat Prinzevalle, interview with author, 15 April 1998.

12. Lawrence A. Greenfeld et al., "Violence by Intimates: Analysis of Data on Crimes by Current or Former Spouses, Boyfriends, and Girlfriends" (report, Washington, D.C., 1998), 14.

13. Phillips, "The Girls Report," 46−47.

14. City of Chicago Department of Public Health, "Prevalence of Domestic Violence among Women Attending Chicago Department of Public Health Clinics" (report, Chicago, 1995), 6.

15. Anara Guard, "Violence and Teen Pregnancy" (report, Newton, Mass., 1997), 2.

16. City of Chicago, "Prevalence of Domestic Violence," 6.

17. Child Trends, "New Research," 1.

18. Phillips, "The Girls Report," 46.

19. Christian Molidor and Richard M. Tolman, "Gender and Contextual Factors in Adolescent Dating Violence," *Violence against Women* 4, no. 2 (1998): 185−93.

20. Maura O'Keefe and Laura Treister, "Victims of Dating Violence among High School Students: Are the Predictors Different for Males and Females?" *Violence against Women* 4, no. 2 (1998): 209−21.

21. Peter Passell, "Economic Scene: A Report Shows How Hard It Is to Break Welfare Dependency," *New York Times*, 31 July 1997, sec. C.

22. Roye and Balk, "The Relationship of Partner Support," 88, 92.

23. Joan Haldeman, author interview, 30 September 1997.

24. Bassuk et al., "Characteristics and Needs," 645.

25. Elizabeth A. Stanko et al., "Counting the Costs: Estimating the Impact of Domestic Violence in the London Borough of Hackney" (report, London, 1997), 6.

26. Carol Goertzel, author interview, 30 September 1997.

27. Stanko et al., "Counting the Costs," 45.

CHAPTER NINE

1. Bray, *Unafraid of the Dark*, 16.

2. Greenfeld et al., "Violence by Intimates," 4.

168

3. Lloyd, "Effects of Domestic Violence," 153.

4. Wilt et al., "Female Homicide Victims," 16.

5. Heise, "Violence against Women," 274.

6. Meier, "Domestic Violence," 223–27. For a recent manifestation of this creed, see Germaine Greer, The Whole Woman (New York: Knopf, 1999), 296. Greer argues that there is no point in trying to establish reasons for men's hatred of women because hatred is irrational. "A woman trying to understand men's cruelty to women is confronted again by a simple antipathy, which is what sexism means."

7. Crenshaw, "Mapping the Margins," 103.

8. Meier, "Domestic Violence," 232–37.

9. Pam Belluck, "A Woman's Killer Is Likely to Be Her Partner, a Study Finds," New York Times, 31 March 1997.

10. Walby, Theorizing Patriarchy, 136.

11. Raphael, "Prisoners of Abuse," 6–10; Riger and Krieglstein, "Impact of Welfare Reform."

12. Brush, "Battering," 8.

13. Gerald T. Hotaling and David B. Sugarman, "An Analysis of Risk Markers in Husband to Wife Violence: The Current State of Knowledge," Violence and Victims 1, 101–24 as quoted in Riger and Kriglstein.

14. Laura Ann McCloskey, "Socioeconomic and Coercive Power within the Family," Gender and Society 10, no. 4 (1996): 457.

15. Anita Raj et al., "Prevalence and Correlates of Relationship Abuse among a Community-Based Sample of Low-Income African-American Women," Violence against Women 5, no. 3 (1999): 285–88.

16. Lindberg et al., "Age Differences," 64.

17. Olive Schreiner, Women and Labour (reprint; London: Virago Press, 1978), 242.

18. Amina Mama, "Woman Abuse in London's Black Communities," in Inside Babylon: The Carribean Diaspora in Britain (London: Verso, 1993), 133–34.

19. Greer, The Whole Woman, 134.

20. Betty Friedan, "Incorporating Men into the Women's Movement," Georgetown Journal on Fighting Poverty 3, no. 1 (1995): 26.

21. Conversation with Lisa Brush, 9 August 1999.

22. McCloskey, "Socioeconomic," 459.

23. Gilligan, Violence, 236–37.

24. Jorge Fitz-Gibbon and Cory Siemaszko, "Ex-Lover Says Slayer Isolated and Beat Her," New York Daily News, 16 February 1996.

25. See Meier, "Domestic Violence," 230–37, for a detailed analysis of this possible synthesis. See also Riger and Krieglstein, "Impact of Welfare Reform."

26. Jason DeParle, "Behind a Welfare Success Story, Struggles," New York Times, 20 April 1999, sec. A.

Bibliography

Abma, Joyce Anne Driscoll, and Kristin Moore. "Young Women's Degree of Control over First Intercourse: An Exploratory Analysis." *Family Planning Perspectives* 30, no. 1 (1998): 12–18.

Abramovitz, Mimi. *Regulating the Lives of Women: Social Welfare Policy from Colonial Times to the Present.* Boston: South End Press, 1988.

Amott, Teresa L. "Black Women and AFDC: Making Entitlement out of Necessity." In *Women, the State, and Welfare,* 280–98. Madison: University of Wisconsin Press, 1990.

Anderson, Elijah. *Streetwise: Race, Class, and Change in an Urban Community.* Chicago: University of Chicago Press, 1990.

Barusch, Amanda, et al. "Understanding Families with Multiple Barriers to Self-Sufficiency." Report, Salt Lake City, 1999.

Bassuk, Ellen, et al. "The Characteristics and Needs of Sheltered Homeless and Low-Income Mothers." *Journal of the American Medical Association* 276, no. 8 (1966): 640–46.

Beck, Joan. "Nation Must Stem the Tide of Births Out of Wedlock." *New Orleans Times-Picayune,* 6 March 1993, section B.

Belenky, Mary Field, et al. *Women's Ways of Knowing: The Development of Self, Voice, and Mind.* New York: Basic Books, 1986.

Belluck, Pam. "A Woman's Killer Is Likely to Be Her Partner, a Study Finds." *New York Times,* 31 March 1997.

Blank, Rebecca M. *It Takes a Nation: A New Agenda for Fighting Poverty.* New York: Russell Sage Foundation, 1997.

Blankenhorn, David. *Fatherless America: Confronting Our Most Urgent Social Problem.* New York: Basic Books, 1995.

Brandwein, Ruth A. *Battered Women, Children, and Welfare Reform.* Thousand Oaks, Calif.: Sage, 1999.

Bray, Rosemary L. *Unafraid of the Dark.* New York: Random House, 1998.

170   Brown, Lyn Mikel, and Carol Gilligan. *Meeting at the Crossroads: Women's Psychology and Girls' Development*. Cambridge, Mass.: Harvard University Press, 1992.

Browne, Angela, and Shari S. Bassuk. "Intimate Violence in the Lives of Homeless and Poor Housed Women: Prevalence and Patterns in an Ethnically Diverse Sample." *American Journal of Orthopsychiatry* 67, no. 2 (1997): 261–78.

Browne, Angela, Amy Salomon, and Shari S. Bassuk. "The Impact of Recent Partner Violence on Poor Women's Capacity to Maintain Work." *Violence against Women* 5, no. 4 (1999): 393–426.

Brush, Lisa D. "Battering, Traumatic Stress, and Welfare-to-Work Transition." *Violence against Women*, forthcoming.

———. "Family Violence and Control as Obstacles to Self-Sufficiency: Perceptions of Rapid Attachment Participants in Allegheny County, Final Report #2," Pittsburgh, 1998.

Campbell, Jacquelyn C., et al., "The Influence of Abuse on Pregnancy Intention." *Women's Health Issues* 5, no. 4 (1995): 214–23.

Center for Social Work Research. "Good Cause Temporary Waivers and Modifications for Victims of Domestic Violence." Report, San Antonio, 1999.

Chant, Sylvia. "Gender and Tourism Employment in Mexico and the Philippines." In *Gender, Work, and Tourism*. London: Routledge, 1997.

Chapman, Stephen. "Target Practice: Conservatives Are Being Attacked by All Sides For 'Trampling on the Poor,' but in the End They Will Be Vindicated." *Chicago Tribune*, 24 September 1995.

Child Trends, Inc. "New Research: Latest State-Level Data Available on Teen Sexual Behavior, Pregnancy, and Births." Report, Washington, D.C., 1997.

City of Chicago Department of Public Health. "Prevalence of Domestic Violence among Women Attending Chicago Department of Public Health Clinics." Report, Chicago, 1995.

Coley, Rebekah Levine, and P. Lindsay Chase-Lansdale. "Adolescent Pregnancy and Parenthood: Recent Evidence and Future Directions." *American Psychologist* 53, no. 2 (1998): 152–66.

Cooley, Tracy, et al., "Safety and Self-Support: The Challenge of Welfare Reform for Victims of Domestic Abuse." Report, Bangor, 1997.

Crenshaw, Kimberle Williams. "Mapping the Margins: Intersectionality, Identity Politics, and Violence against Women of Color." In *The Public Nature of Private Violence*, 93–118. New York: Routledge, 1994.

Curcio, William. "The Passaic County Study of AFDC Recipients in a Welfare-to-Work Program: A Preliminary Analysis." Report, Paterson, N.J., 1997.

Danziger, Sandra, et al. "Barriers to the Employment of Welfare Recipients." Paper presented at the Association for Public Policy Analysis and Management Conference, New York City, October 1998.

Davis, Martha F., and Susan J. Kraham. "Protecting Women's Welfare in the Face of Violence." *Fordham Urban Law Journal* 22 (1995): 1141–57.

DeParle, Jason. "Behind a Welfare Success Story, Struggles." *New York Times*,   171
20 April 1999, section A.

———. "Shrinking Welfare Rolls Leave Record High Share of Minorities."
New York Times, 27 July 1998, section A.

Dobash, R. Emerson, and Russell L. Dobash. *Women, Violence, and Social Change.*
New York: Routledge, 1992.

———. *Violence against Wives.* New York: Free Press, 1979.

Dutton, Mary Ann. *Empowering and Healing the Battered Woman: A Model for Assessment and Intervention.* New York: Springer, 1992.

Dutton, Mary Ann, et al. "Battered Women's Cognitive Schemata." *Journal of Traumatic Stress* 7, no. 2 (1994): 237–55.

Edin, Kathryn, and Laura Lein. *Making Ends Meet: How Single Mothers Survive Welfare and Low Wage Work.* New York: Russell Sage Foundation, 1997.

Ferris, Mrs. A. "When It Pays Not to Work." Letter to the editor of the *Daily Telegraph*, 15 December 1997.

Figueredo, Aurelio Jose, and Laura Ann McCloskey. "Sex, Money, and Paternity: The Evolutionary Psychology of Domestic Violence." *Ethology and Sociobiology* 14 (1993): 353–79.

Fineman, Martha. *The Neutered Mother, The Sexual Family, and Other Twentieth Century Tragedies.* New York: Routledge Press, 1995.

Fitz-Gibbon, Jorge, and Cory Siemaszko. "Ex-Lover Says Slayer Isolated and Beat Her." *New York Daily News*, 16 February 1996.

Friedan, Betty. *The Feminine Mystique.* New York: Dell, 1963.

———. "Incorporating Men into the Women's Movement." *Georgetown Journal on Fighting Poverty* 3, no. 1 (1995): 25–27.

Friedmann, John. *Empowerment: The Politics of Alternative Development.* Oxford: Blackwell, 1992.

Gambetta, Diego. "Primo Levi's Plunge: A Case against Suicide." *New York Times*, 7 August 1999, section A.

Gelinas, Denise J. "The Persisting Negative Effects of Incest." *Psychiatry* 46, no. 4 (1983): 312–32.

Geronimus, Aline T. "Teenage Childbearing and Personal Responsibility: An Alternative View." *Political Science Quarterly* 112, no. 3 (1997): 405–30.

Gerston, Jill. "Television: Big Hospitals, Strong Women, Prime Time: A Former Moll Flanders Joins the Surgical Staff." *New York Times*, 15 February 1998, section 2.

Gilligan, James. *Violence: Our Deadly Epidemic and Its Causes.* New York: Punam, 1996.

Ginn, Kate, and Barbara Davies. "My Undying Love for Man Who Shot Me." *Daily Mail*, 12 November 1997.

Gladwell, Malcolm. "Six Degrees of Lois Weisberg." *New Yorker*, 11 January 1999, 52–63.

172   Gordon, Linda. *Heroes of Their Own Lives: The Politics and History of Family Violence.* New York: Viking Press, 1988.

————. *Pitied but Not Entitled: Single Mothers and the History of Welfare, 1850–1935.* New York: Free Press, 1994.

Greenfeld, Lawrence A., et al. "Violence by Intimates: Analysis of Data on Crimes by Current or Former Spouses, Boyfriends, and Girlfriends." Report, Washington, D.C., 1998.

Greer, Germaine. *The Whole Woman.* New York: Knopf, 1999.

Guard, Anara. "Violence and Teen Pregnancy." Report, Newton, Mass., 1997.

Haennicke, Sheila B., et al. "Trapped by Poverty, Trapped by Abuse, Supplement I." Report, Chicago, 1998.

Harlow, Caroline Wolf. "Female Victims and Violent Crime." Report, Washington, D.C., 1991.

Hartmann, Heidi, and Roberta Spalter-Roth. "Reducing Welfare's Stigma: Policies That Build upon Commonalities among Women." *Connecticut Law Review* 26 (1994): 901–12.

Heilbrun, Carolyn G. *Writing a Woman's Life.* New York: Norton, 1998.

Heise, Lori L. "Violence against Women: An Integrated, Ecological Framework." *Violence against Women* 4, no. 3 (1998): 262–90.

Herman, Judith. *Trauma and Recovery.* New York: Basic Books, 1992.

Hines, Richard Davenport. *Auden.* New York: Pantheon Books, 1995.

Horizon Research Services. "Focus Group Participants: Clients of Women's Employment Network." Report, Columbia, Mo., 1996.

————. "Focus Group Participants: Social Workers and Employers." Report, Columbia, Mo., 1996.

Ibrahim, Farah A., and Edwin L. Herr. "Battered Women: A Developmental Life-Career Counseling Perspective." *Journal of Counseling and Development* 65, no. 5 (1987): 244–48.

Institute on Violence. "Violence in the Lives of African-American Women: A Focus Group Study." Report, New York, 1996.

Jaffe, Peter G., and David A. Wolfe. *Children of Battered Women.* Newbury Park, Calif.: Sage, 1990.

Jones, Ann. *Next Time She'll Be Dead.* Boston: Beacon Press, 1994.

Jones, Dan, and Associates. "Domestic Violence Incidence and Prevalence Study." Report, Salt Lake City, 1997.

Kane, Thomas J. "Giving Back Control: Long-Term Poverty and Motivation." *Social Science Review* 61, no. 3 (1987): 405–19.

Kanuha, Valli. "Domestic Violence, Racism, and the Battered Women's Movement in the United States." In *Future Interventions with Battered Women and Their Families,* 34–50. Thousand Oaks, Calif.: Sage, 1996.

Kenney, Catherine T., and Karen R. Brown. "Report from the Front Lines: The Impact of Violence on Poor Women." Report, New York, 1996.

Kirkwood, Catherine. *Leaving Abusive Partners: From the Scars of Survival to the* 173 *Wisdom of Change.* London: Sage, 1993.

Kunerth, Jeff. "She Got a Job and His Abuse." *Orlando Sentinel,* 21 December 1997.

Lebowitz, Leslie, Mary R. Harvey, and Judith Lewis Herman. "A Stage-by-Dimension Model of Recovery from Sexual Trauma." *Journal of Interpersonal Violence* 8, no. 3 (1993): 378–91.

Lennett, Judith. "Children of Domestic Violence." Report, Boston, 1996.

Lewin, Tamar. "Americans Are Firmly Attached to Traditional Roles for Sexes, Poll Finds." *New York Times,* 27 March 1996.

Lewis, Oscar. "The Culture of Poverty." In *On Understanding Poverty.* New York: Basic Books, 1968.

Lindberg, Laura Duberstein, et al. "Age Differences between Minors Who Give Birth and Their Adult Partners." *Family Planning Perspectives* 29, no. 2 (1997): 61–66.

Lloyd, Susan. "The Effects of Domestic Violence on Women's Employment." *Law and Policy* 19, no. 2 (1997): 139–67.

Lloyd, Susan, and Nina Taluc. "The Effects of Male Violence on Female Employment." *Violence against Women* 5, no. 4 (1999) 370–92.

Luker, Kristin. *Dubious Conceptions: The Politics of Teenage Pregnancy.* Cambridge, Mass.: Harvard University Press, 1996.

McCloskey, Laura Ann. "Socioeconomic and Coercive Power within the Family." *Gender and Society* 10, no. 4 (1996): 449–63.

McCormack Institute and Center for Survey Research. "In Harm's Way? Domestic Violence, AFDC Receipt, and Welfare Reform in Massachusetts." Report, Boston, 1997.

McKinnon, John D. "Battered Wife Challenges Denial of Jobless Benefits." *Wall Street Journal,* 30 July 1997.

McWilliams, Monica. "Violence against Women in Societies under Stress." In *Rethinking Violence against Women.* Thousand Oaks, Calif.: Sage, 1998.

Mama, Amina. "Woman Abuse in London's Black Communities." In *Inside Babylon: The Carribean Diaspora in Britain,* 97–136. London: Verso, 1993.

Massey, Douglas, and Nancy Denton. *American Apartheid: Segregation and the Making of the Underclass.* Cambridge, Mass.: Harvard University Press, 1993.

Masters, Brook A. "Mother Slain a Day after Seeking Help." *Washington Post,* 28 May 1998, section A.

Mead, Lawrence M. *From Welfare to Work: Lessons from America.* London: The Institute of Economic Affairs, 1997.

———. *The New Politics of Poverty: The Nonworking Poor in America.* New York: Basic Books, 1992.

Meier, Joan. "Domestic Violence, Character, and Social Change in the Welfare Reform Debate." *Law and Policy* 19, no. 2 (1997): 205–63.

174   Miller, Kim S, Leslie F. Clark, and Janet S. Moore. "Sexual Initiation with Older Male Partners and Subsequent HIV Risk Behavior." *Family Planning Perspectives* 29, no. 5 (1997): 212–14.

Molidor, Christian, and Richard M. Tolman. "Gender and Contextual Factors in Adolescent Dating Violence." *Violence against Women* 4, no. 2 (1998): 180–94.

Morin, Richard, and Megan Rosenfeld. "With More Equity, More Sweat: Poll Shows Sexes Agree on Pros and Cons of New Roles." *Washington Post*, 22 March 1998, section A.

Mott, Frank L. "When Is a Father Really Gone? Paternal-Child Contact in Father-Absent Homes." *Demography* 27, no. 4 (1990): 499–517.

Murphy, Patricia A. *A Career and Life Planning Guide for Women Survivors: Making the Connections Workbook.* Delray Beach, Fla.: St. Lucie Press, 1995.

———. "Recovering from the Effects of Domestic Violence: Implications for Welfare Reform Policy." *Law and Policy* 19, no. 2 (1997): 169–82.

Murray, Charles. *Losing Ground: American Social Policy, 1950–1980.* New York: Basic Books, 1984.

Musick, Judith S. *Young, Poor, and Pregnant: The Psychology of Teenage Motherhood.* New Haven, Conn.: Yale University Press, 1993.

Nelson, Jill. *Straight, No Chaser: How I Became a Grown-up Black Woman.* New York: Putnam Penguin, 1997.

Newman, Katherine S. *No Shame in My Game: The Working Poor in the Inner City.* New York: Knopf and the Russell Sage Foundation, 1999.

Nussbaum, Martha C. *Sex and Social Justice.* New York: Oxford University Press, 1999.

Ohio Domestic Violence Network. "Study on Economic Status of Women in Domestic Violence Populations: January 1997." Report, Columbus, 1997.

O'Keefe, Maura, and Laura Treister. "Victims of Dating Violence among High School Students: Are the Predictors Different for Males and Females?" *Violence against Women* 4, no. 2 (1998): 195–223.

Orloff, Ann. "Gender and the Social Rights of Citizenship: The Comparative Analysis of Gender Relations and Welfare." *American Sociological Review* 58, no. 3 (1993): 303–28.

Page, Clarence. *Showing My Color.* New York: HarperCollins, 1996.

Passell, Peter. "Economic Scene: A Report Shows How Hard It Is to Break Welfare Dependency." *New York Times*, 31 July 1997, section C.

"Pat's Story." Report, Salt Lake City, 1996.

Pearson, Jessica Nancy Thoennes, and Esther Ann Griswold. "Child Support and Domestic Violence: The Victims Speak Out." *Violence against Women* 5, no. 4 (1999): 427–48.

Phillips, Lynn. "The Girls Report: What We Know and Need to Know about Growing Up Female." Report, New York, 1998.

Plichta, Stacey. "Violence and Abuse: Implications for Women's Health." In   175
Women's Health: The Commonwealth Fund Survey, 237–70. Baltimore: Johns Hopkins
University Press, 1996.

Pollack, Wendy, and Martha F. Davis. "The Family Violence Option of the
Personal Responsibility and Work Opportunity Reconciliation Act of 1996: In-
terpretation and Implementation." *Clearinghouse Review* 30, no. 11 (1997):
1079–98.

Popenoe, David. *Life without Father: Compelling New Evidence That Fatherhood and
Marriage Are Indispensable for the Good of Children and Society.* New York: Free Press,
1996.

Quayle, Dan, and Diane Medved. *The American Family.* New York: HarperCollins, 1996.

Raj, Anita, et al. "Prevalence and Correlates of Relationship Abuse among a
Community-Based Sample of Low-Income African-American Women." *Violence
against Women* 5, no. 3 (1999): 272–91.

Raphael, Jody. "Domestic Violence and Welfare Receipt: Toward a New
Feminist Theory of Welfare Dependency." *Harvard Women's Law Journal* 19,
(1996): 201–27.

———. "Domestic Violence: Telling the Untold Welfare-to-Work Story."
Report, Chicago, 1995.

———. "The Family Violence Option: An Early Assessment," *Violence against
Women* 5, no. 4 (1999): 449–66.

———. "Prisoners of Abuse: Domestic Violence and Welfare Receipt."
Report, Chicago, 1996.

———. "Prisoners of Abuse: Policy Implications of the Relationship between Domestic Violence and Welfare Receipt." *Clearinghouse Review* 30, no. 3
(1996): 186–94.

Raphael, Jody, and Richard M. Tolman. "Trapped by Poverty/Trapped by
Abuse: New Evidence Documenting the Relationship between Domestic Violence and Welfare." Report, Chicago, 1997.

Raphael, Jody, and Sheila Haennicke. "Keeping Battered Women Safe
through the Welfare-to-Work Journey: How Are We Doing? A Report on the
Implementation of Policies for Battered Women in State Temporary Assistance
for Needy Families (TANF) Programs." Report, Chicago, 1999.

Richie, Beth E. *Compelled to Crime: The Gender Entrapment of Battered Black Women.*
New York: Routledge, 1996.

Riger, Stephanie, and Maryann Krieglstein. "The Impact of Welfare Reform
on Men's Violence against Women," *American Journal of Community Psychology*,
forthcoming.

Riger, Stephanie, et al. "Obstacles to Employment of Welfare Recipients
with Abusive Partners." Report, Chicago, 1998.

Roberts, Dorothy E. "The Value of Black Mothers' Work." *Connecticut Law
Review* 26 (1994): 871–78.

176   Salomon, Amy, Shari S. Bassuck, and Margaret G. Brooks. "Patterns of Welfare Use among Poor and Homeless Women." *American Journal of Orthopsychiatry* 66, no. 4 (1996): 510–25.

Schreiner, Olive. *Women and Labour.* Reprint. London: Virago Press, 1978.

Sev'er, Aysan. "Recent or Imminent Separation and Intimate Violence against Women: A Conceptual Overview and Some Canadian Examples." *Violence against Women* 3, no. 6 (1997): 566–89.

Shepard, Melanie, and Ellen Pence. "The Effects of Battering on the Employment Status of Women." Report, Duluth, n.d.

Sidel, Ruth. *Keeping Women and Children Last.* New York: Penguin Books, 1996.

Simon, David, Joe Nawrozki, and Gary Cohn. "Loving Father's Tragic Solution." *Baltimore Sun,* 18 September 1995, section A.

Spalter-Roth, Roberta A., and Heidi Hartmann. "Dependence on Men, the Market, or the State: The Rhetoric and Reality of Welfare Reform." *Journal of Applied Social Sciences* 18, no. 1 (1994): 55–70.

Stanko, Elizabeth A. *Intimate Intrusions: Women's Experience of Male Violence.* London: Unwin Hyman, 1985.

Stanko, Elizabeth A., et al. "Counting the Costs: Estimating the Impact of Domestic Violence in the London Borough of Hackney." Report, London, 1997.

Stark, Evan, and Anne Flitcraft. "Personal Power and Institutional Victimization: Treating the Dual Trauma of Woman's Battering." In *Post Traumatic Therapy and Victims of Violence,* ed. Frank M. Ochberg, 115–51. New York: Brunner/ Mazel, 1988.

Stewart, Abigail J. "Discovering the Meaning of Work." In *The Experience and Meaning of Work in Women's Lives.* Hillsdale, N.J.: Lawrence Erlbaum Associates, 1990.

Tjaden, Patricia, and Nancy Thoennes. "Stalking in America: Findings from the National Violence against Women Survey." Report, Denver, 1997.

Tolman, Richard M., and Daniel Rosen. "Domestic Violence in the Lives of Welfare Recipients: Implications for the Family Violence Option." Paper presented at the Association for Public Policy Analysis and Management Conference, New York City, October 1998.

Tomasky, Michael. *Left for Dead: The Life, Death, and Possible Resurrection of Progressive Politics in America.* New York: Free Press, 1996.

U.S. Public Law 104–193, 104th Cong., 2d sess. 1996.

Virginia Department of Social Services. "A Summary of Responses from Local Departments of Social Services to a Questionnaire on Domestic Violence." Unpublished memorandum. Richmond, Virginia, n.d.

Walby, Sylvia. *Theorizing Patriarchy.* Oxford: Blackwell, 1990.

White, Lucie. "No Exit: Rethinking 'Welfare Dependency' from a Different Ground." *Georgetown Law Journal* 81 (1993): 986–90.

Whitehead, Barbara Dafoe. "Dan Quayle Was Right." *Atlantic Monthly*, April 1993, 47–84.

Wilson, William Julius. *The Truly Disadvantaged: The Inner City, the Underclass, and Public Policy*. Chicago: University of Chicago Press, 1987.

Wilt, Susan A., Susan M. Illman, and Maia Brody Field. "Female Homicide Victims in New York City, 1990–1994." Report, New York City, 1997.

Wingood, Gina M., and Ralph J. DiClemente. "The Effects of an Abusive Primary Partner on the Condom Use and Sexual Negotiation Practices of African-American Women." *American Journal of Public Health* 87, no. 6 (1997): 1016–18.

Woolf, Virginia. *The Diary of Virginia Woolf*. New York: Harcourt Brace Jovanovich, 1978.

———. *A Room of One's Own*. New York: Harcourt Brace Jovanovich, 1957.

———. *Moments of Being: Unpublished Autobiographical Writings*. Sussex: University Press, 1976.

———. *The Virginia Woolf Reader*. San Diego: Harcourt Brace, 1984.

Yilo, Kersti, and Murray A. Straus. "The Impact of Structural Inequality and Sexist Family Norms on Rates of Wife-Beating." *Journal of International and Comparative Social Welfare* 1 (1984): 16–29.

Index